As
Baba Lon

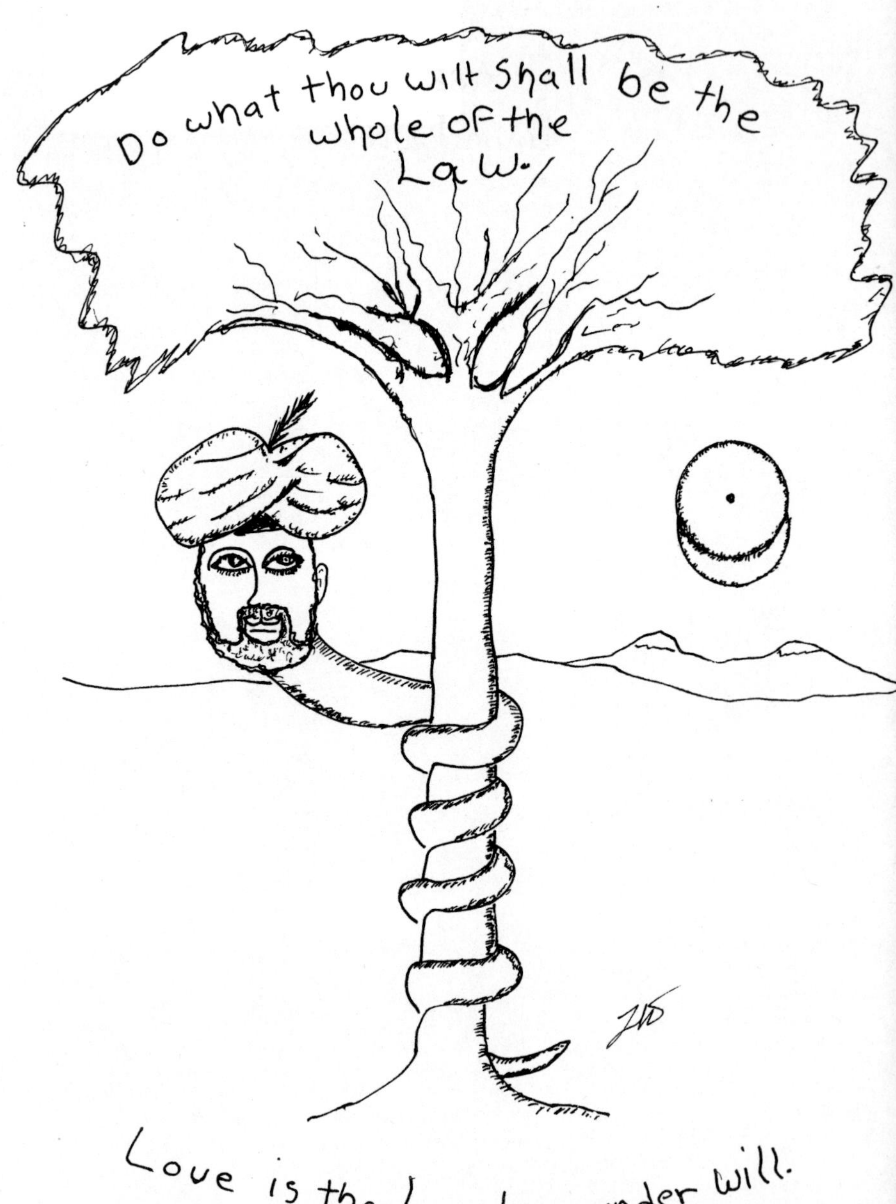
Do what thou wilt shall be the whole of the Law.
Love is the law, love under will.

Ask Baba Lon

Answers to Questions of Life and Magick

by

Lon Milo DuQuette

New Falcon Publications
LAS VEGAS, NEVADA, U.S.A.

Published in 2011 by:
NEW FALCON PUBLICATIONS
9550 S. Eastern Avenue • Suite 253
Las Vegas, Nevada 89123
www.newfalcon.com
info@newfalcon.com

ISBN-13: 978-1-56184-219-3
ISBN-10: 1-56184-219-2

Book Design and Production by Studio 31
www.studio31.com

Printed in the USA

This little collection
of interviews and letters
is dedicated to

PHYLLIS SECKLER
(1917–2004)

the first magician to answer *my* letters.

Everything I say's untrue,
Though true I try to make it.
As soon the word escapes my lips,
Would I have never spake it.

Baba Lon

Contents

Angels & Demons,

The Holy Guardian Angel

Real Life

Miscellaneous Technical Matters

Reincarnation

Acknowledgements

The author wishes to recognize and thank the following friends, colleagues, and muses whose love, encouragement, and support has made this labor of love possible: Constance Jean DuQuette, Jean-Paul DuQuette, Patty Smith, David Cherubim, Jonathan Taylor, Rick Potter, Judith Hawkins-Tillirson, Janet Berres, Thomas Caldwell, Kent Finne, Kat Sanborn, Jim Wasserman, Vanese Mc Neil, Chance Gardner, Liz Guerra, John Boye, Gini Martini, Ariel Sirocco, Thalassa Therese, Glenn Turner, Anastasia S. Haysler, Marcus Katz, Tali Goodwin, Amanda Mary Catherine Hanson, Kelly and Angela Landrith, Margo Adler, Donald Michael Kraig, and Rodney Orpheus.

I would especially like to voice my most sincere thanks to Michael Miller of New Falcon Publications, whose father, Dr. Alan Miller (Christopher S. Hyatt), gave me my first professional writing experience and opportunities. I am thrilled that Michael is determined to carry the publishing torch that was so courageously borne by his late father, and I am proud to continue to be associated with this important and historic publishing house.

Disclaimer

Let it be understood that when writing as Baba Lon or Lon Milo DuQuette, I am voicing my opinions. In this little book I am not acting as a spokesperson or representative of any organization, magical or fraternal order, society or church. My opinions are entirely my own and sometimes at odds with those of my colleagues and superiors for whom I have the utmost love and respect.

I also confess that where I believe it to be necessary I have taken the liberty to edit the content of some of the letters to protect the privacy and identity of my correspondents. I have also in certain instances combined the text of two or more of my responsive letters which address similar or identical questions.

Invocation of the Turban

I am a man, like any man,
With feet of clay and cheeks of tan.
But when I wrap my turban on
The Gods are near.
I'm Baba Lon.

I eat too much. I drink too much,
A greedy, selfish such-and-such.
But when I wrap my turban on
My mind is clear.
I'm Baba Lon.

A lazy coward, vain and violent,
Chatter on when I should stay silent.
But when I wrap my turban on
I have no fear.
I'm Baba Lon.

I'm mean and cruel like Genghis Khan,
Spend too much time with the TV on.
But when I wrap my turban on
Great Truths appear.
I'm Baba Lon.

Introduction

Who Is Baba Lon?

When I wrap my turban on
The Gods are near. I'm Baba Lon.
—from *Invocation of the Turban*

Writing is a presumptuous profession. Do you actually believe I talk like this in everyday conversation? I don't. The moment my fingers start tapping away at the keyboard, falsehoods pour onto the page, and whatever pathetic glints of honest mental clarity I may temporarily possess are immediately smothered in crapulous affectations.

There! See what I mean? *"honest mental clarity"*—*"pathetic glints"*—*"crapulous affectations"* … Do you actually think I go around the house dropping phrases like that? Not bloody likely! It's all such a charade! (I hope you heard me lugubriously drawl the word *"charaaaaahde"* with an affected proper posh British accent … *daawling.*)

But what can I do? As a writer I'm never alone. There is always an unseen ear listening to my voice, and long as there is an audience I'm going to play to it. It can't be avoided. And so it would be eminently fair for you to ask me how I can play to the audience and still present a genuine Lon.

A few years back, after having written a half-dozen books on magick and other such matters, I took it in my head to write a book on practical Qabalah. It's a subject around which much controversy swirls. Because I am a house-and-garden variety *practical* qabalist and not an orthodox *speculative* qabalist, I knew I was going to have to be especially careful to avoid treading on sensitive traditional toes. I was not looking forward to having to do so by applying yet another layer of pretense to my work.

But then it occurred to me that I could step on all the toes I wanted to if I wrote the book *pseudepigraphically.* (Don't worry. I had to look it up too. It means I wrote the book pretending I was someone else.) Stuff like that was done all the time in classical Jewish literature. I'd sit down and create an outrageous, very *un*orthodox rabbi who gave voice to my true and un-sanitized views. With brash impunity the rabbi could say all the things that might be too dangerous for me to say. Then, playing the role of occult author Lon Milo DuQuette (mild-mannered, objective and dispassionate observer), I could introduce the good rabbi's material to the world and offer my dispassionate and conservative comments. As two people I would also have many opportunities to call myself a genius.

My publisher bravely agreed to the idea, so I set to work. I had no idea it would be such a liberating experience. Like a tongue-tied adolescent who becomes brash and eloquent when he dons a mask, or like the ventriloquist who lets his dummy vent his inmost feelings, I discovered another person inside myself—a person who was only too happy to tell me what I really thought about things—a person whose primary audience was *me*—a voice to speak to *my* ear.

The book you are about to read was written by another one of those *me*s inside of me. I call him *Baba Lon* for a number of reasons, the first and most important being I like the sound of it. It's fun to push the words out of my mouth—*"Baba Lon."* Secondly, it is obviously a play on the name *Babalon,* the great goddess of the magical and Thelemic pantheon.

In India *baba* means *father* and is a term of endearment usually applied to sadhus or other religious personages. As I grow older I become more and more comfortable with the role of a Baba. I like the idea of being the avuncular and irascible character who answers letters with ruthless candor and writes profane* and edgy notes and poems—the person who squiggles his own visage in books and greeting cards—the person who aims his thoughts person-to-person, one shot at a time, to anyone who, for one reason or another, feels the need to … *Ask Baba Lon.*

Over the years lots of people have taken the time to write and do just that; and (probably more times than was wise) Baba Lon has taken the time to answer. Early on I started to save and file these exchanges. I guess in the back of my brain I always thought that perhaps someday (when I'm in my dotage) I could organize them into a little book for the amusement and edification of magicians (and students and teachers of magick). It finally occurred to me (at the age of sixty-two) that time better be now. What I didn't expect, however, was how much I would be amused and edified by the project. I can affirm without hesitation that, in the course of organizing this material, this jaded old wizard has learned more about magick, mysticism, and myself than I ever dreamed was possible at this season of life.

As you will soon discover, some of the letters I receive are much longer than my responses. This is because Baba Lon is at heart a lazy correspondent and often preoccupied with other matters vital to keeping a roof over his head. But before you dismiss all of these brief replies as simply flippant retorts, please know that before I pop a letter in the mail box or hit the 'send' button I often spend many hours distilling pages of my rambling initial responses into precisely what I believe is the most efficient answer.

Finally, I want to remind the reader that the letters and interviews that comprise the text of *Ask Baba Lon* were written over a period of many years, and that I may or may not still

* I hope the reader will forgive the informality of the 'voice' I use in responding to some of these letters. I confess I am a vulgar man and from time-to-time consummately comfortable slipping into profanity.

completely agree with my answers of a decade or two ago. Indeed, I often find myself in the afternoon disagreeing with my morning's opinions. So, while I hope my thoughts and magical opinions will be helpful to your own meditations and work, I want you to always remain mindful that …

Everything I say's untrue,
Though true I try to make it.
As soon the word escapes my lips,
Would I have never spake it.

Baba Lon

Magazines Ask Baba Lon

Before we plunge into the esoteric madness of the individual letters to and from Baba Lon, I thought that the reader who might not already be familiar with my life and work might benefit from the following answers to some very generic questions posed over the years by magazine interviewers from around the world. I've selected three such interviews for this section of the book and hope they will yield maximum 'bang' for your *Ask Baba Lon* 'buck.'

✺

Interview With American Magician Lon Milo DuQuette

[Note: This interview is from about ten years ago. The Russian interviewer had recently read the manuscript for my novel, *Accidental Christ.**]

M: The first question would be this: Did you know Anton LaVey? If yes, can you tell me your impressions of him? He seemed demonic and dark. However, according to everything I read about you, you are a very optimistic and pleasant person to be with.

Can you tell us more about your personality?

LMD: I never met LaVey, though I know a few people who did. All of them were favorably impressed by his intelligence and (believe it or not) his humor. He artfully used (through

* Lon Milo DuQuette, *Accidental Christ – The Story of Jesus as Told by His Uncle* (Chicago, IL: Thelesis Aura, 2007).

a kind of shock therapy) his "dark" and "demonic" image to help people free themselves of their unhealthy religious programming. I certainly do not mean in any way to denigrate the memory of LaVey, but I do not view him as an occultist per se. He was a delightful and colorful slap in the face of all religious hypocrisy. He helped many people "snap out" of the coma of original sin and other unnecessary and unwholesome religious programming. He was a great showman and he did his job very well and with great style. I miss him.

M: What is the usual day of a modern magician? Do you start it with some spells, curses, and magical tricks as some common people think?

LMD: When you think about it, all life is magick and everything we do is ritual. Whether we know it or not, we are all magicians twenty-four hours a day. We are either competent or incompetent practitioners of our craft. I have made my ordinary life magick and my magick life ordinary. The act of putting on my socks is no less magical than the act of invoking Thoth or penetrating the 10th Enochian Aethyr.

As a young magician my daily routine included many of the colorful activities you would expect from a fledgling wizard: morning and evening ritual work, yoga, pranayama, meditative exercises, experimental spirit evocations, and various kinds of divinatory practices (Tarot, I Ching, Geomancy, etc.). I had no idea why I was doing any of these things. I just knew that they were part of the magician's training program, and assumed that someday this training would come in handy.

Now my days are pretty normal. My wife, Constance, wakes me up by passing a cup of magick potion (hot coffee) under my slumbering nose. After drinking about half of it, I remember who I am and what must be done. The first thing that must be done is to pay the rent and put food on the table. To assure this happens on a regular basis, five days a week I perform an extended nine-hour magical ritual I call "going to work." (Holding a real job is one of the two most impressive magical feats I have ever accomplished. The most impressive is my blissful thirty-four-year marriage to Constance.)

People ask me how I find time to write, practice magick, and work full-time. To tell you the truth, if I had all day to write I don't think I would write one word more than I do now. (And I know I wouldn't be able to pay the rent!) I'm the type of lazy person that needs to trick myself into believing that I'm a competent and productive individual. I need to get up, get dressed, go out into the world and cheerfully mix with people who would burn me at the stake if they knew what I did and what I believed. I need to balance the bizarre world of the magician with what others call "objective reality." The "normal" world helps me to "ground" my magick, and my magick energizes my "normal" world. Over the years I've observed that magicians who are unable to balance these two worlds are in very grave danger. First, they lose their sense of humor; then they lose their minds.

Yesterday was a good example of the contrasts in my life. As I drove to work (in my rusty old 1977 Volkswagen camper), I performed my morning devotions to the Hindu God Ganesha by chanting His Holy Name 108 times to the tune *of Pop Goes the Weasel.* I honor this God (who is the remover of obstacles) because 1) I look like him, and 2) He continues to arrange that my supervisor does not realize that I am the worst worker in her department. (I've written my last four books at work.)

Yesterday morning was pretty typical. I sat at my computer and processed some paperwork and chatted three times on the telephone with my publisher. At lunch I wrote 400 words of a new book, and then went back to pushing papers. I know ... it doesn't sound very magical, does it?

The evening was more of what you might expect of a practicing magician. Around 8:00 p.m. my house filled with local magicians who gathered to help us celebrate the Feast of the *Three Days of the Writing of The Book of the Law*. The ceremony began when Constance lit a huge bowl of fire (while reciting a lovely enchantment from Crowley's Rite of Mars: "*I swear by Djinn and by Shin and by the space between that I will not stir from this place until the fire of God hath flamed upon the water that is upon the altar* ...", *etc.)*. Then, with the flames dancing wildly, I stepped to the altar and celebrated Crowley's *Mass of the Phoenix*, which entails the act of slashing a certain symbol into my chest with a magical knife. (I do this only one night a year ... it's very bloody. Everyone seems to love it!) ... Sound more magical?

M: It was astonishing for me to read your words: "*Short as it is, Accidental Christ took me a little over twelve years to complete. During that time, as I followed the discoveries brought to light by Dead Sea Scroll research, I was repeatedly amazed to learn that many of the elements of background and character that I penned purely from my imagination were, in fact, verified by modern scholarship.*"

How can you explain this? Is this intuitive thinking a feature of Art in general, or is there something in the human mind that allows people to "see" things?

Was there anything else revealed to you during your writing experience?

Could the process of writing be a tool that helps us to learn about a reality?

LMD: I absolutely believe that writing is excellent medicine for the mind and soul. The writer is required to reduce things to their essence and deal with them on the spot (exactly what a magician does when he or she evokes a spirit). I think that is very good for one's mental health.

I don't think I was channeling anything (or anyone) more mysterious than myself when I wrote *Accidental Christ*. At times I was simply a bit more "awake" to what should have been obvious to scholars and theologians of the past had they been armed with a better understanding of political, social, and religious realities of first century Palestine.

M: What do you think about Aleister Crowley's literary talent?

LMD: It was immense. His output was absolutely astounding. People often make fun of his poetry because it is so esoteric and, often, so shocking. As for his novels ... well ... I don't know if I'm an objective critic when it comes to his novels. Let me ask you something. Have you ever read a novel written by someone you know very well—a good friend or a relative? If you have, I bet that it was very difficult for you to enjoy it, because you know the creator so well that it is almost impossible to suspend your disbelief. That's how I feel about Crowley's *Moon Child* or *Diary of a Drug Fiend.* If I didn't know so much about Crowley, these books might be very engaging. As it is, I can't help but second-guess his motives and I feel the embarrassment that a close friend might feel who is confronted with his comrade's literary pretensions. Does this make any sense?

I believe Crowley's best works are his Class A—Holy Books. These are of a class of spiritual literature comparable only to Blake, Ezekiel or John. They can't be analyzed with the intellect. They are word-pictures ... images morphing like a Brownian movement into other images. These works are Crowley at his best, although he did not take credit for writing any of them.

M: What brought you into literature?

LMD: It's a little scary to hear my work being called *literature.* In my early 40s I more or less woke up to the fact that there might be other people who were interested in what I considered the most important things in life—things that, because of my passion for magick, I knew a little something about.

In 1988, my good friend, Christopher Hyatt, was kind enough to ask me to write an epilogue to his book, *Secrets of Western Tantra.*[*] That was the first thing I ever had published. We discovered that we worked very well together and he generously asked if I would be interested in co-authoring a book about Sex Magick, Tarot and the Holy Guardian Angel. I said, "Sure!" We didn't stop there. In the next two years, he and I co-authored four books that I'm happy to say have been very well received.

M: Would you like to write something else similar to *Accidental Christ*?

LMD: There appears to be some interest in having *Accidental Christ* turned into a motion picture. I'll believe that when I see it. Nevertheless, to placate certain friends, I've promised to produce a screenplay adaptation. If I really believed that I had enough time left, I would love to write an exposé of Paul. I *really* don't like that guy.

M: What are your plans?

LMD: My new book, *The Chicken Qabalah of Rabbi Lamed Ben Clifford*[†], will be out this summer, and I'm well into the next book after that. (I've been asked not to comment on that one quite yet). In August, I'll be traveling to Oslo and London and teaching at the Omega Institute in New York.

---

* Christopher S. Hyatt, Ph.D., *Secrets of Western Tantra.* (Scottsdale, AZ: New Falcon Publications, 1989. Third revised edition, 2009).

† Lon Milo DuQuette, The Chicken Qabalah of Rabbi Lamed Ben Clifford: Dilettante's Guide to What You Do and Do Not Need to Know to Become a Qabalist (York Beach, ME: Weiser Books, 2001).

M: Do you think that your knowledge of Sex Magick could help you to write a good pornographic novel?

LMD: Probably not. Sex Magick is highly erotic, but the "magick" takes place on internal planes of consciousness. I'm afraid that a viable Sex Magick novel would not capture the imagination of an avid fan of pornography, and that a commercially viable pornographic novel would disappoint a serious student of Sex Magick.

M: Does this knowledge help you in your personal life?

LMD: I love sex. I love magick. This knowledge *is* my personal life. Sometimes it helps. Sometimes it doesn't.

M: How do historical discoveries and research—similar to the Dead Sea Scrolls findings—influence Magick? What kind of interaction could be between Technology and Magick in the future?

LMD: These are excellent questions. Every new discovery—historical, astronomical, medical, mathematical, or scientific—changes humanity and the magical formulae that help us get things done. Crowley's new Aeon of Horus will not be a *new* Aeon forever. Every new discovery mutates *who* we are—*what* we are. Just think about how different our lives are from those of our parents, and their parents. My grandfather rode a horse and defecated in a hole in the ground. His community had no electricity, no indoor plumbing, no telephones, no airplanes, no Pluto, no black holes, no DNA. It's impossible to talk to my mother about religion or magick, not because she is stupid but because we come from two different worlds.

The same will hold true with the next generation of magicians who will arm themselves with the tools of biotechnology to instantly induce levels of consciousness we old wizards had to struggle to comprehend and achieve.

Yes, I think the magick of the future—perhaps the very near future—will be incomprehensibly magnificent.

✺

America's Occultist: An Interview with Lon Milo DuQuette

Patheos.com* April 5, 2010. Interviewer, Star Foster

SF: With fifteen books on magick and the occult, your duties in the O.T.O., your lectures and appearances as a guest expert on TV and radio, you seem to stay busy. What projects are you currently working on?

LMD: I have a new book coming out in November (from Llewellyn) titled *Low Magick—It's All in Your Head, You Just Have No Idea How Big Your Head Is.*† It's autobiographical and contains stories of magical operations I've done over the years. The title is a bit tongue-in-cheek, facetiously using the term

---

* From their website: "Founded in 2008, Patheos.com is the premier online destination to engage in the global dialogue about religion and spirituality, and to explore and experience the world's beliefs. Patheos is the website of choice for the millions of people looking for credible and balanced information or resources about religion. Patheos brings together the public, academia, and the faith leaders in a single environment, and is the place where people turn to on a regular basis for insight into questions, issues, and discussions. Patheos is unlike any other online religious and spiritual site, and is designed to serve as a resource for those looking to learn more about different belief systems, as well as participate in productive, moderated discussions on some of today's most talked about and debated topics.

† Lon Milo DuQuette, *Low Magick—It's All in Your Head, You Just Have No Idea How Big Your Head Is* (St. Paul, MN: Llewellyn Publications, 2010).

"Low Magick" to refer to any magical operation one actually performs rather than those one just talks or argues about.

I'm also finishing up a new book called *Ask Baba Lon*. I've been working on this one for over twenty years. It is a collection of letters I've received over the years from magicians (and would-be magicians) and my answers back. Some are absurd and funny, but most are extremely good questions and observations that required me to really search my soul in order to discover what I really think about these matters.

SF: You've been with the Ordo Templi Orientis for over thirty years and have served as its US Deputy Grand Master since 1996. What initially drew you to the O.T.O., and what do you think is the most interesting aspect of the organization today?

LMD: I didn't know it at the time, but there were only five or six members of the O.T.O. (surviving from Crowley's day) still living when I wrote my first letter of inquiry to the Order back in 1973. I had read a couple of things by Aleister Crowley and heard a lot of things (mostly bad) about him; but I just had a feeling that despite his bad reputation, this colorful character was a real holy man. As it turns out, the more I discover about him the greater is my conviction that this is true.

In my opinion, the most interesting aspect of the organization today is the demonstrable success of its mission of perpetuating the works of Aleister Crowley and the propagation of Thelema as a bona fide spiritual philosophy. In addition to this, the O.T.O. provides the very real magical experiences of its various degree initiation ceremonies, which I believe to be among Crowley's greatest magical rituals.

SF: You're also an Archbishop in the Ecclesia Gnostica Catholica. Can you tell us a little bit about the E.G.C. and its relationship to the O.T.O.?

LMD: Ecclesia Gnostica Catholica (E.G.C.) is the ecclesiastical arm of the O.T.O. It is *not* a separate organization. It is *not* a separate spiritual entity. This puts us in a similar position as our traditional ancestors, the Knights Templar, who were a military secret society independent of King and Church. They were answerable only to the Pope (who seldom questioned anything they did) and they had their *own* priests and their *own* confessors. In other words, like the O.T.O., they had their own church within the Order.

Get used to thinking of the O.T.O. and E.G.C. as the exact same organization viewed with different glasses. Put on your O.T.O. glasses and you see the O.T.O. with our Frater Superior, our Supreme and Holy King or Queen, our Sovereign Grand Inspectors General, our Most Wise Sovereigns, our Lodge Masters, and members of the various degrees (some of whom have volunteered for extra duties). Put on your church glasses and look at the same thing and you see the E.G.C. with our Sovereign Patriarch or Matriarch, our Presiding Bishop, our Bishops, and our Priestesses, Priests and Deacons.

SF: Most people don't think of magical disciplines as spirituality. Is there a difference between a magical discipline and a spiritual discipline?

LMD: I guess it depends entirely on the attitude, motive, and intent of the individual practitioner. It's quite possible, in my opinion, to be a perfectly effective magician without subscribing to any particular discipline that most people usually consider as being "spiritual".

SF: You were on a Pagan panel at PantheaCon recently. Many Pagans are interested in the O.T.O., especially through the writings of Crowley and yourself, although the O.T.O. itself isn't specifically Pagan. How would you characterize the relationship of the O.T.O. and the Pagan community? Do you consider yourself Pagan?

LMD: It, of course, comes down to your accepted definition of the word "Pagan." If by the term you mean "rustic" or "country person," I am not a Pagan. If by the term you mean a person that reveres or worships a deity or pantheon of deities other than that (or those) worshipped by the Abrahamic religions, then my answer is a qualified "Yes."

However, if you are asking if I'm a person who worships the earth as the supreme goddess and attempts to synchronize my entire spiritual focus upon the rhythms of the year and its cycles of agriculture and husbandry, my answer is an unqualified "No." I don't worship the "Pagan" goddess of nourishment of two aeons ago. I don't worship the "Chrislemew (Christian Moslem or Jew) dying god of sacrifice and superstition of the last aeon. If anything, I worship the Child that represents the formulae of the present aeon, and I attempt to synchronize my spiritual focus on the formula of natural growth. If that makes me a Pagan… then I'm a Pagan.

SF: Can someone be active in the O.T.O. without being a member of the Thelemic religion? Are all faiths welcome?

LMD: The O.T.O. requires only that an individual be able to say in good conscience that he or she "accepts *The Book of the Law* (the primary Holy Book of Thelema, dictated to Crowley by a praetor-human intelligence in 1904) without wishing to make changes in it." As no one may presume to interpret *The Book of the Law* for another, this puts the responsibility for one's understanding of the text squarely in one's own lap. If an individual believes that his or her religious beliefs can be compatible with his or her understanding (or even *indifference* as to the meaning) of *The Book of the Law*, then there is no other litmus test other than that applied by the individual.

That being said, there are many O.T.O. members who consider themselves Pagans. There also quite a few who consider themselves Jews. One of my dearest O.T.O. brothers is a Moslem. There are even those who consider themselves Christian (although by most "Christian" doctrinal standards they would be considered highly irregular or even heretical Christians). There are quite a few who are comfortable identifying themselves as atheists, and a growing number who are Freemasons who are vocally NOT atheists.

SF: Much of Ceremonial Magick draws from Judeo-Christian traditions. For some Pagans that's uncomfortable territory. Why should a Pagan work with angels or study Jewish mysticism?

LMD: They shouldn't feel the need to if they are comfortable with their mastery of the rites and traditions of their Pagan religion.

SF: The O.T.O. has been associated with Sex Magick and you have written three books on the subject. What would you like to say to people who are interested in Ceremonial Magick and the O.T.O., but find the subject of Sex Magick uncomfortable or off-putting?

LMD: If after reading what I've written about the subject, someone is still disturbed by a discussion of the more universal or even metaphoric aspects of sex, then I must respectfully conclude he or she has important psychological issues that should be addressed before becoming involved in ANY form of esoteric study undertaken by adults.

SF: Your acclaimed book on practical Qabalism for the magical community, *The Chicken Qabalah of Rabbi Lamed Ben Clifford: Dilettante's Guide to What You Do and Do Not Need to Know to Become a Qabalist*, is written in the voice of an imaginary rabbi. Why did you choose to write as a humorous fictional character?

LMD: Because Rabbi Lamed Ben Clifford could say things that I would be hesitant to say. It's like the shy ventriloquist who can only really speak his heart through the wooden lips of his dummy.

SF: Your autobiography, *My Life with the Spirits**, is required reading for two classes at DePaul University in Chicago. Can you tell us about that?

LMD: It's a class on Modern Religion. A few years ago when I was in Chicago I even got to address the class.

SF: Magical authorities, like Crowley, have traditionally been seen as self-aggrandizing and egotistical, and magical texts as obscure and ciphered. Your autobiography and books on magick tend to be funny and down-to-earth. Is humor and accessibility necessary to reach a modern audience?

LMD: Probably not for everybody. It is how I see things, so it is how I attempt to communicate.

SF: Do you think information on magical and spiritual matters can be too readily available?

LMD: No.

SF: Aleister Crowley, undisputed as a talented occultist, delighted in his nefarious reputation and claimed to have lived quite a wild life. You've written several books on Crowley's work. Do you have an opinion of the man himself? Was he as wicked as he made himself out to be?

---

* Lon Milo DuQuette. *My Life with the Spirits: The Adventures of a Modern Magician*. (York Beach, ME: Weiser Books, 1999).

LMD: He didn't just claim to have a wild life ... he had a wild life! No wilder perhaps than a Ramakrishna, or an Oscar Wilde, or Timothy Leary, however.

Let me ask you this. Have you ever met and tried to have a friendship or a business relationship with a great artist (a famous novelist, or film maker, or actor, or dancer, or choreographer, or composer, or virtuosic musician, or singer, or poet, or painter, or sculptor) who is also a bona fide genius? It may start out pleasant enough, but more often than not the more you become enmeshed in their mad world the more your world is turned upside down.

It's not always the case, but many times these people can be almost dangerously unstable ... they can be real jerks! Cruel and sarcastic prima donnas who focus so much on their art that they can be completely oblivious to the feelings, well-being, or even safety of those around them. They are filled with shortcomings and character flaws and hang-ups, because they've just never had a normal life to work these issues out and frankly they don't care. Their art is the magical object of the operation that is *their lives*—not you, not the press, not even history. Crowley, I believe, was such a person. There are aspects of his life that I applaud—that awe me—that touch me in ways that only inspired spiritual literature can. Then, there are ample examples of the man being petty and cruel. Frankly, I don't think I would have long been comfortable in his presence. His "wickedness" was no more wicked than the shortcomings of any artist/genius. The difference is that Aleister Crowley's "wickedness" was part of his art.

SF: Your autobiography, *My Life with the Spirits*, contains a few cautionary tales of your early days of practicing magick. What advice would you give someone beginning a magical discipline?

LMD: Don't be afraid. It's good to be wise. It's good to be cautious. But it's never good to be afraid. Never. If you make a mistake … big deal! You'll live through it (most likely). It's better to do something and make a mistake than to *not* do something because you are afraid of making mistakes.

SF: You've written a lot about classical magical systems. What do you think of Chaos Magick?

LMD: I think if I were a youngster starting my study of magick it would be a very attractive introduction to the art.

SF: What do you think has been the most important contribution to Ceremonial Magick in the past fifty years?

LMD: The personal computer, the Internet, and quantum physics.

SF: What do you think the future holds for Ceremonial Magick?

LMD: A longer past.

SF: Looking back on your life, what reward, if any, have your years of magical practice and study given you?

LMD: This might seem too simple and corny, but my biggest "reward" has been a certain success in achieving a measure of (what I presumptuously will call) "enlightened happiness". Maybe it's all been merely a matter of good luck. But who knows for sure what luck really is?

SF: Many of our readers may not know you're also a musician. Your country-rock band from the early 70s, Charley D. and Milo, is being rediscovered by a new generation and you've been busy independently recording original folk songs.

Any plans to release, or re-release, any of your music as a CD or EP?

LMD: I'm so glad you asked. Yes. Before I wrote books I wrote songs, and for a while made a pretty good living at it. I gave music and recording a rest for twenty-five years, but have picked it up again in the last couple of years (maybe it's just my fourth or fifth midlife crisis). In the last couple of years I've been (again) lucky enough play some local clubs in the LA area and to book concerts in the U.S., Japan, and Australia. Even back in the 70s my music was magical in nature (Charley and I called it *acid cowboy*). I've recently made a couple of CDs (just me and my guitar) of my songs of sloppy sentiment, offensive blaspheme, and diabolic Americana. I beg everyone reading this to buy them: *The White Album* (so named because I couldn't afford color) and *The Black Album*. You can get them fastest through the following website: http://kunaki.com/MSales.asp?PublisherId=110456. Please do this before you think about it. It will be easier that way.

Remember, I'm not asking anyone to listen to these CDs but I would appreciate it if you bought them!

SF: Possibly your most remarkable magical act is being married to your lovely wife, Constance, for over forty years. Any secrets to successful matrimony you'd like to share?

LMD: Try not to get to know each other very well. Communication is way overrated, and mystery remains an aphrodisiac.

✷

An Interview with Lon Milo DuQuette
AbraHadAbra—
The Magickal Observer Magazine* (Germany)

AHA: Lon Milo DuQuette is a magician, expert, Thelemite, author, elocutionist. How does [your] private life work if [you are] always on the run with Thelema?

LMD: My private life works pretty well. Constance and I have been married since 1967. We live in a cozy little place in Costa Mesa, California, and keep pretty busy with life. We both travel (I more than she). Our son and his family live in Japan.

AHA: As an American you are living in a country where several cultures meet. How do you experience the daily cultural life, the relations people have?

LMD: In America I don't have too many opportunities to closely encounter many of the local foreign cultures. There are many Mexicans (California was part of Mexico). This is a wonderful place for food! I love Japanese, Chinese, Vietnamese, Thai, Indian, Greek, Italian, etc. That's perhaps the best part of living with so many cultures around.

AHA: Barack Obama recently became the first African American to be elected President of the United States; he was inaugurated as the forty-fourth president on January 20, 2009. Millions of people in the United States and also here in Germany set great hope in Obama and the expectations are giant. But there are also skeptics like Noam Chomsky who beg

* ISSN: 2190-1724, March 21, 2009. Olaf Francke. Publisher/ Interviewer. Neidthard Kupfer, editor. Used with permission.

to differ [and believe] that Obama doesn't want or won't be able to fulfill these expectations. What kind of expectations do you attach to the election of Barack Obama for the forty-fourth president of the United States? Do you think Obama can hold the promise of "change" or do you think skeptics like Chomsky are right?

LMD: Oh, probably a little of both. We certainly needed to get rid of the Bush international crime family and Dick Cheney. I believe Obama is an extraordinary individual and we need an extraordinary person at this time. I know it's impossible for him to fulfill all my expectations but I believe he will do as well as anyone in this situation.

AHA: At the moment the world markets are moving into a serious recession. What is your opinion in this case?

LMD: Capitalism has failed. Communism has failed. I think the old way of looking at money is going to have to radically change. I think we're in for a very bumpy ride.

AHA: At the same time we see worldwide terrorism, which is the reason for restrictions to individual citizens' rights to defeat danger. Wars are made to oppose terrorism. Do you support these measures? Are there any alternatives?

LMD: Do I support these measures? No. Are there any alternatives? Yes. The alternatives are common sense and the respect for human dignity.

AHA: How should the world be?

LMD: Interesting and inspiring.

AHA: If you had to go to a lonely island and you were allowed to take three things with you, which things would be that?

LMD: 1) A copy of the I Ching; 2) A good ukulele; 3) Sunscreen.

AHA: Lon Milo DuQuette, you are a Thelemite. What is a Thelemite?

LMD: The generic Thelemite is anyone who has realized the importance of discovering his or her true will and is attempting to live it.

AHA: How did you become a Thelemite?

LMD: By striving to discover my purpose in life and then doing it.

AHA: Does your family support your way of life?

LMD: My father and mother are dead. Everyone else is very supportive.

AHA: How long have you been a member of the Ordo Templi Orientis?

LMD: Since November 15, 1975.

AHA: Has your membership in the O.T.O. changed you in a positive or negative [way]?

LMD: Very positive.

AHA: In the U.S.A. the O.T.O. is a noteworthy active community, which is perceptible in a number of MySpace accounts. The American Thelemites are open for new things and they are very present. In Germany there are only a few Thelemites (who identify themselves as such with their MySpace photo and name). What do you think, Lon Milo? What's the reason, and what can we do to change this?

LMD: I think people truly come to Thelema only when they are ready. I don't try to convert people by any other means than by the example of my life.

AHA: Do you think it is better to teach Thelema as an Arcanum, or should it be performed as a movement?

LMD: It will unfold how it will unfold.

AHA: Do you think that Thelema and religion belong together? If yes, in which way?

LMD: I cannot speak for any other Thelemite. For me, Thelema is my religion, my philosophy, my Way.

AHA: You are an author of many interesting books, also on Thoth Tarot. This tarot clearly distinguishes itself from other decks. What do you think is this deck exactly?

LMD: I believe it is a wonderful example of the evolution of Qabalah-based Tarot.

AHA: What is the difference between Thoth Tarot and other decks?

LMD: That is a big question. I wrote an entire book trying to answer it. Please read my book, *Understanding Aleister Crowley's Thoth Tarot* (there is a German translation) for that answer.

AHA: On Atu XI (Lust) we see BABALON riding the Beast, holding the grail. We have an elaboration of Olaf Francke from 2005, which says Atu XI shows a beginning pregnancy; the grail is a zygote in the uterus. What do you think about that?

LMD: Sounds reasonable.

AHA: Aleister Crowley was an important person for the 93 Current. What would you like to say to him face-to-face?

LMD: Can I borrow your wand?

AHA: In your Thoth Tarot book, published in Germany in 2005, it is written that you first thought Crowley was a Satanist and that you discovered more about him later. Today Crowley is identified as a "founder of modern Satanism."* What do you think about Crowley today?

LMD: Today I see Crowley as a true modern Holy Man.

AHA: An author from Switzerland wrote about Crowley in 2007, that he was a "magical ne´er-do-well, unprincipled and weak, rascal, woman violator." In this book Crowley is also titled as a *fascist*.† What would you reply to those statements?

LMD: He was a bit of all of the above ... except he was not a fascist!

AHA: Crowley was the head of your order. Are you proud of that? Why?

LMD: Yes. It's always interesting and enlightening to have a prophet, Holy Man, and genius as the head of an organization.

AHA: Do you think that Crowley was a prophet of the New Aeon? Did Crowley found the aeon?

LMD: Yes; no.

AHA: In Germany there are those that say Crowley received the *LiberAL vel Legis* in 1904 in a very shorter form than known now. Perhaps he expanded *The Book of Law* in 1909/1910 while

* *Akrons Crowley Tarot Führer,* Vol.1, p. 37.

† *Ibid.* p. 56.

he was working on the *Liber 418* and *777* and brought it into a more Qabalistic form (220 Verses [22x10], 65 Pages [ADNI] and so on). What do you think about this theory?

LMD: With the exception of the paraphrased verses from the stele, which were added later, I believe it is as originally dictated.

AHA: Can you say exactly who may be the owner of the original script of the *Liber AL Vel Legis*, and if it would be available for scientific examination?

LMD: I believe it is in the O.T.O archives. I'm not the person you need to talk to about examination.

AHA: And now, finally, is there anything more you want to say to the readers of our magazine?

LMD: Thanks for the opportunity to chat. Do what thou wilt shall be the whole of the Law. Love is the law, love under will.

Thelema, Aleister Crowley, A∴A∴ *and* O.T.O.

"Do what thou wilt shall be the whole of the Law."*

"Love is the law, love under will."†

These two phrases should be familiar to modern magicians and those familiar with the life and works of Aleister Crowley. They are the watchwords of the religious and/or philosophic movement known as "Thelema".

Much of the material in *Ask Baba Lon* was written in response to questions concerning Thelema, Thelemic magick, the work of Aleister Crowley, and the two magical societies that he led. This reflects the level of interest expressed by a large number of my correspondents, many of whom, having read those of my books that treat directly or indirectly on Crowley's life and magick, still have unanswered questions or otherwise wished to make a point.

I'd like to point out that in the final years of his life, Crowley was organizing his own version of *Ask Baba Lon* which he initially wanted to title, "Aleister Explains Everything." An edition of this work was finally published (posthumously) and given the title, "*Magick Without Tears.*"‡ I am given to understand that a new, more complete edition of this

---

* *Liber AL vel Legis* (The Book of the Law), Chapter I, Verse 40. The use of the salutations, "Do what thou wilt shall be the whole of the Law" *and* "Love is the law, love under will" are used by Thelemites when greeting each other and parting. Many of the letters in this section originally began and ended with these words. For editorial brevity I have omitted their use in most letters reproduced in *Ask Baba Lon*.

† *The Book of the Law* Chapter I, Verse 57.

‡ Aleister Crowley, *Magick Without Tears* (Scottsdale, AZ: New Falcon Publications, 1991).

marvelous work is in the editorial stages and will eventually be available. I urge anyone who is interested in Crowley's work to obtain a copy.

Magick Without Tears is absolutely brilliant and I recommend it especially to people just starting out their study of Crowley and Thelema. Its singular shortcoming, however, is that it contains only Crowley's letters and not those of his correspondents. We are left to guess the nature of the original questions that prompted his responses. *Ask Baba Lon* contains both sides of the conversation, and though I've taken great editorial pains to correct spelling and protect the identities of the writers, the letters that prompt my replies are for the most part left intact.

I've made only a token attempt to organize the letters into neat little categories, such as magical orders, O.T.O./A.∴A.∴/Golden Dawn, *The Book of the Law*, etc., as all these facets of Thelema and magick blend into one another (often in the same paragraph). I must also point out that much of the correspondence in other sections of the book also deal directly or indirectly with Crowley, Thelema, and O.T.O./A.∴A.∴ matters, so please don't think that I have exhausted my comments on these subjects in this first section.

But before we get to the individual letters, I thought you might be interested in how Baba Lon went about explaining the Great Beast, Aleister Crowley, to a class of junior high school students. That is precisely what I had the opportunity to do several years ago when I was asked by a young student to be interviewed as part of his school's History Day class project.

✺

Aleister Crowley—History Day Class Project

Dear Baba Lon,

My name is (name withheld) and I am doing a History Day project at my school about Aleister Crowley. If you could please answer the following questions for me, I would greatly appreciate it.

[A list of questions was submitted]

Thank you very much.

Name withheld.

....

Dear Name withheld,

I have to say you have chosen a very interesting and historic character to write about for your History Day project. In 2002, the BBC conducted a poll of 30,000 Britons, asking them to vote for the person who was, in their opinion, the "Greatest Briton of All Time." Named number seventy-three in the top one hundred (sandwiched between King Henry V and Robert Bruce) stands the "famous poet, author and philosopher, Aleister Crowley."

I'm happy to answer your questions. Here you go.

1. What do you consider Aleister Crowley's legacy for modern culture?

Crowley's legacy for modern culture would be impossible to itemize and even less possible to prove. But let's look at it this way. Did the Beatles change the consciousness of western civilization in the 1960s? Did the revolution in human thought that characterized that period in history profoundly affect the music, art, fashion, movies, food, literature, philosophy, science, religion, and politics of today? Unless you've been living in a state of complete denial, a coma, or a cave, the answer is, "Yes!"

Crowley's life, works, and philosophies influenced not only John Lennon of the Beatles, Mick Jagger of the Rolling Stones, Jimmy Page of Led Zeppelin, and David Bowie; they also influenced scores of other cultural icons, such as visionary writers Ray Bradbury, Arthur C. Clark, William Burroughs and Robert Heinlein, and film-makers Orson Wells, Kenneth Anger, and George Lucas. And let's not forget rocket scientist Jack Parsons, a founder of the Jet Propulsion Laboratory (the predecessor of NASA) and the inventor of jet-powered take off. Parsons was a space pioneer, who is honored with a crater on the moon named after him. He was also a personal student of Aleister Crowley.

This is only one part of Crowley's legacy for modern culture. Crowley's ideas change people; these people changed, and are continuing to change, the world.

2. What are the three most important aspects of his legacy?

i.) His revolutionary spiritual view that the True Will of each individual is the same thing that in the past has been labeled the "Will of God."

ii.) His ethical view that discovering (and then doing) one's True Will is the only way to truly gain enlightenment and advance human consciousness and evolution.

iii.) His philosophy that says, in essence, that no one can define Truth for another person.

3. Of all of Aleister Crowley's works, which do you think has had the most influence today?

*The Book of the Law** (*Liber AL vel Legis*)—a book that Crowley channeled in 1904 in Cairo which forms the basis of his work. It's a very strange little book. One might think at first reading that it makes little sense at all.

4. What misconception about Aleister Crowley would you like to be cleared up the most?

The most absurd and vicious slander still repeated today is the false accusation that Crowley advocated and/or participated in human sacrifice. This accusation is totally untrue and based upon the most ignorant and ill-informed interpretations of some of his more esoteric writings.

5. In your opinion, what was the most widely believed misconception of Aleister Crowley?

That he was a "Satanist" or a "Black Magician." The fact that he developed such a horrible reputation is mostly his own fault, because many times when he was accused of such things he didn't bother to deny them, thinking intelligent people would see through such absurdities. Unfortunately, most people weren't (and still aren't) as intelligent or well-informed as he assumed.

6. If Aleister Crowley were alive today how would people view him? Would it be different or close to the same as in the 1800s and at the turn of the 20th century?

I believe Crowley was born just about sixty years ahead of his time. Most people today who really do their homework about

* Aleister Crowley, *The Book of the Law* (York Beach, ME: Weiser Books, 1976).

the man find him brilliant, funny, and profoundly inspiring. If Crowley were alive today, his lifestyle and attitudes would not seem very shocking or controversial.

7. How did you first know about Aleister Crowley—where and when?

I first saw his picture on the cover of the Beatles' *Sgt. Pepper's Lonely Hearts Club Band* album. Later, I was referred to his works in relation to my study of Hebrew mysticism, Hermetic Qabalah, magick, and Tarot. It seemed I saw his name and references to his work everywhere I turned.

8. Do you think that Aleister Crowley's legacy will ever be forgotten?

His name may eventually be forgotten, but I believe the essence of his legacy is a permanent stone in the pyramid of human spiritual evolution.

9. Why do you think some bands have put his writings/pictures/names in their works?

I imagine some do it to be "spooky" and "satanic," but others do it out of genuine respect for this remarkable and historic character, and see the essential freedom of the human soul that Crowley celebrated reflected in their art.

10. In your opinion, what is the most inspirational book by Crowley?

Liber Tzaddi, a tiny little book that is published among *The Holy Books of Thelema.** I also get endless inspiration from *The*

---

* Aleister Crowley, *The Holy Books of Thelema* (York Beach, ME: Weiser Books, Inc., 1983).

*Book of Thoth,** an extended commentary on the Tarot which he wrote toward the very end of his life.

Thanks for giving me this opportunity.

My best to you and your parents, and good luck with your class project.

Baba Lon

✺

I Want to Convert My Local Church Leaders to Thelema!

[Note: For the purpose of illustration I have left the spelling, punctuation, and grammar uncorrected.]

Dear Baba Lon

Do What Thou Wilt, Shall Be The Whole Of The Law.

I have read Crowley's letter to Henry Ford and his *Method of Thelema,* which seems to indicate that it is necessary to promulgate the law, by writing to industrialists, bankers, scientists and politicians and the likes. (I would include to the leaders of local old aeon churches) The idea being to persuade them using example from their own fields, be it mathematical proofs or biblical scriptures than (sic) support the Law of Thelema and show it has solid foundation and practical benefits.

* Aleister Crowley, *The Book of Thoth by The Master Therion: A Short Essay on the Tarot of the Egyptians* (London: O.T.O., 1944); The Equinox II (5), reprint, (York Beach ME: Samuel Weiser, 1992).

Why is it that I get so much opposition when I do this from both the recipient of my letter as well as from other Thelemites who claim such letters hurt the cause?

Love Is The Law, Love Under Will.

Name withheld

....

Dear Name withheld,

Let me begin by pointing out the correct punctuation and capitalization of "Do what thou wilt shall be the whole of the Law." As found in *Liber AL vel Legis (The Book of the Law.)*

By the wording in your letter it is unclear to me if you are contacting great industrialists, bankers, scientists, and politicians, or if you are writing only to leaders of your local old aeon churches. I'm assuming that you are mostly engaged in contacting the latter. Forgive me if I'm mistaken.

I don't know the reason you are getting "opposition" to this idea from other Thelemites, but everyone is, of course, entitled to his or her own view on the matter. I think it's a good idea in principle and, in application, a worthy effort for a knowledgeable and eloquent champion of Thelema who truly believes himself or herself up to the task of winning over—through charm, tact, logic and common sense—a person who has completely surrendered logic and common sense to dedicate his or her life to the soul-suicide insanity that is the very essence of Chrislemew (Christian, Moslem, and Jewish) thought.

Rubbing their noses in how stupid they are probably won't win them over. That's why Crowley mentioned industrialists, bankers, scientists and politicians and the likes—because *these* people, while many of them may be assholes, *are NOT stupid*! Their success and their power prove they are likely at least 90 percent Thelemite to start with. They are people who have proven they know how to (at least on the material plane) discover and do their Will. Their success in causing change to occur in conformity with their Will makes them pretty damned good magicians too!

That's who Crowley wanted to go after—powerful individuals who, if properly approached, would be brilliant enough to recognize a good thing when they see it—not some loser clergymen or will-less spider-professors preaching to the choir of their same ilk in their sunless cloisters.

The big fish are not caught with a net of mathematical proofs or qabalistic arguments of old-aeon scripture, but are drawn into the greater sea by the impulse of their own Will. That is most likely to happen if they find themselves attracted to Thelema by a successful and compelling example of a Thelemite they admire—someone they might wish to emulate.

These, of course, are only my personal opinions ... and my opinions can change many times an hour. If you are being criticized for your efforts, try to be honest with yourself and consider what your critics are saying (or trying to say) to you. But if you truly can't see the wisdom in the criticism and know yourself to be right, then fuck 'em! I doubt you can ultimately "hurt the cause" of Thelema too badly.

Love is the law, love under will.

Baba Lon

P.S. Again, please note the proper capitalization and punctuation of our Thelemic greetings taken from *Liber AL vel Legis*. If you are going to do intellectual combat in the cause of Thelema against the Chrislemew clergy you might want to emblazon your battle standard with a correctly spelled slogan.

✵

Do You Have to Practice Magick to Be a Thelemite?

Dear Baba Lon,

I was introducing a friend of mine to some Thelemic work a few days ago, and he asked a question I didn't see a clear answer to: "Sooo ... do you have to practice magick to be a Thelemite?" I mentioned that a Thelemite is one who accepts the Law and is actively pursuing the discovery of one's True Will. The comedic difficulty came in his response: "Oh, alright. Then what's the real point of doing it? I mean I like Thelema but I don't see a reason to go through all this really hard material to find my True Will. And then you have the whole hierarchy thing with the A∴A∴ and the O.T.O."

I explained, of course, that the Great Work can be done as an individual, just as you said. However, I was still left with that inability to understand how oftentimes difficult study (Qabalah, Enochian, and just about any other practice with its heavy doses of symbolism) is really sensible in finding the True Will. Any advice here?

Thanks in advance.

Sincerely,

Name withheld

....

Dear Name withheld,

In my opinion, in order to personally and privately (though, when you think of it, existence itself is personal and private) consider oneself a Thelemite, it is not at all necessary to practice any of the techniques of magick, belong to any initiatory society, or subscribe to or enmesh oneself in the study any religion, doctrine, or philosophy other than that of seeking to discover, and then do, one's Will.

I think it safe to say that by this definition most people on the planet who are successfully discovering and executing their Wills do not realize (nor do they need to) that they are "Thelemites" or that there is a name for what they are, or that what they are doing is magick of the highest order. It doesn't matter if they consider themselves Christian, Jew, Moslem, or atheist. If they've discovered and are doing their Wills they're really Thelemites deep down. After all, the statement is, "Do what thou wilt shall be the whole of the Law," not "*Know* what thou wilt ..." or "*Learn* what thou wilt ..." or "*Study* what thou wilt ..." or "*Fantasize* what thou wilt ..." or "*Identify oneself* as thou wilt ..."

That being said, it is also my opinion that in order to publicly and purposefully (love those "p" words!) identify oneself as a Thelemite and represent oneself as an adherent to the religious philosophy known to the world since 1904 as "Thelema," one need only accept *Liber AL vel Legis, the Book of the Law,* (without wishing to make changes to it) and be engaged in a perpetual process of living life as much as possible according to one's current comprehension of the text.

That being said, it is my opinion that if one perceives it to be one's Will to embark consciously upon the step-by-step path of spiritual initiation—the path followed by aspirants and holy men and women of every age—it is vitally important (as it has always been) to attune the process with the spiritual formula that is presently in harmony with humanity's current level of consciousness. How this is done need not be that difficult. In fact, the easiest way to understand the nature of the present spiritual formula is by studying the formulae of the past as expressed in religious and magical rituals.

This is what connects the *Law of Thelema* to personal initiation and magical practices. One of the greatest gifts

Aleister Crowley bequeathed to humanity is a body of rituals and mystical literature built upon the initiatory formulae of the past but now tweaked to bring them in line with the formula of the New Aeon. To identify as a Thelemite at this level one must be like the Tibetan monk on the path to Lamahood: perform the disciplines, do the homework, study the literature, do the rituals, and *live the life*, until such time as one becomes an integral part, expression, and manifestation of the formula itself.

I hope this has been helpful.

Baba Lon

✷

Can You Sum up Thelema and Crowley for the Layman?

Dear Baba Lon,

How would you describe Thelema to the layman? If I had no occult knowledge, and I was looking into the religion for the first time and asked you to *sum it up* for me, what would you say?

Also, how would you sum up Crowley to those unaware of who he was?

Thank you.

Name withheld

....

Dear Name withheld,

Sum up Thelema and Crowley? Damn! You're not asking for much this morning!

Look. The only thing any of us knows for sure about ourselves is that we currently *exist*, and that we are *here*. Most of us also have an abiding conviction that (for reasons beyond our current ability to comprehend) our present individual existence is somehow a *correct* phenomenon in the greater scheme of things. (Otherwise, why would we struggle so passionately to preserve and prolong our existence?) Are you with me so far?

Without presuming to speculate unduly why we exist, why we are here, or why all this is probably correct, Thelema recognizes each individual's place *in* and potential contribution *to* the universe as a whole. Thelema then goes on to posit that it is the duty of each one of us to discover what our unique potential contribution really is. In Thelema this duty is called "Will." Once we discover what that duty is (or at least get a glimpse of what it might be), it then becomes imperative that we fulfill that duty (just like a planet or an electron in its proper orbit) and make that contribution to the universe of which we are a necessary part. In Thelema we call this, "doing one's Will." Still follow me?

Obviously, discovering and executing our Will can be a difficult process. But so is living a life guided by any other philosophical or religious program. What makes Thelema unique is that it treats the *individual* as the basic unit of society, responsible entirely for his or her own reality. For, as I said, the only thing any of us knows is that we currently exist, and that we are here.

How would I sum up Crowley to those unaware of who he was? I would simply say that Aleister Crowley was an extremely eccentric and controversial holy man of the 20th century. His theories on the nature of human consciousness are viewed by many as mystical pre-echoes of the revelations of modern quantum mechanics and astrophysics. For this his followers hail him as the prophet of the New Aeon.

I hope this has been helpful.

Baba Lon

✵

Will the Real A∴A∴ Please Stand Up?

Dear Baba Lon,

Could you tell me which A∴A∴ you recommend?

Name withheld

....

Dear Name withheld,

There's more than one A∴A∴?

Baba Lon

....

Dear Baba Lon,

I mean which lineage. It's rumored (yes, on the Internet, lol) that some of them aren't living up to their original purpose.

Or can you put me in touch with the right people? I just don't want to get defrauded on something so important; the internet abounds with those who claim to be "The One True Wise Order." Thanks! :)

Name withheld

....

Dear Name withheld,

I knew what you meant. (I was just being a smart-ass.)

When it comes right down to it I don't believe that *anyone* is qualified to say with absolute certainty which "lineage" of A∴A∴ is or is not living up to its original purpose.

If you believe that you are in the A∴A∴ the pressure is really on *you* (and not your A∴A∴ contact) as far as how you go about prosecuting the Great Work. For instance, I know of at least two "lineages" that come from Crowley through Germer through whomever. One of them I consider to be about as legitimate and ethical as any on earth; the other is led by an individual that I personally consider to be mentally ill and perhaps even dangerous.

Of course I wouldn't recommend the latter; not because I'm challenging the individual's A∴A∴ credentials, but because I think he or she is, at the moment, mad as a hatter!

That being said, I am also very uncomfortable with any "group" that actively recruits members by hinting, suggesting or advertising they are the "doorway" to the A∴A∴, or are otherwise "dedicated to the service" of the A∴A∴. Even though leaders of these groups may indeed have "legitimate" personal A∴A∴ credentials, I believe their actions are at best a presumptuous misrepresentation, and at worst a gross perversion of Crowley's original schema for private A∴A∴ work, and the creation of a social environment ripe for all the abuses we commonly associate with cults.

In my opinion the A∴A∴ is a profoundly private affair, and until such time as you are prepared to take on a student you should only officially know one other person—your superior.

At the moment I have no reservations about giving you the address below:

Chancellor
BM ANKH
London WC1N 3XX ENGLAND

At the moment, I trust the source of this information and I have yet to receive a complaint from others with whom I've shared it.

That's about as helpful as I can be at the moment. Good luck.

Baba Lon

✻

Jerks and Assholes in the O.T.O.?

Dear Baba Lon,

I have questions that I hope you may be able to answer for me.

Everything that I have read regarding the Law of Thelema, the O.T.O., and the "93/93" says to me that one must live with integrity and with the aim of living in alignment with one's higher will and divinity. It is saying to me that I should try and control my base will and be disciplined in harnessing the higher.

I know a couple of people that are involved with the O.T.O. and they always seem to escape from life through alcohol and drugs. They do not seem to live lives with morals or with any concern for the well being of others. They just seem hell-bent on pursuing their own fleeting interests, it seems, to the detriment of their own self growth.

I am inquiring as to whether my interpretation of the O.T.O. has some truth to it, and if it does, I am hoping you may be able to suggest where I turn now to investigate further.

Sincerely,

Name withheld

....

Hi Name withheld,

Being a member of the O.T.O. (or any other organization) does not in-and-of itself make one a Thelemite.

You observe accurately that not all (perhaps "most") people who present themselves as Thelemites live up to the standards and ideals you might associate with someone who is seeking to discover and then do his or her Will.

I have been in the O.T.O. since 1975 and I have seen many jerks and assholes come and go. I've seen some transform to great adepts, and I've seen some of them crash and burn—fall by the wayside—and die.

One thing I have learned in all these years is that it is a big mistake for me to spend too much of *my* precious time trying to guess or verify to my satisfaction whether or not this Brother or that Sister is behaving *Thelemic-ly.*

Give me a break! Who the fuck am *I* to judge whether or not someone is living up to the Thelemic ideal? I have a hard enough time determining from moment-to-moment whether or not *I* am behaving Thelemic-ly.

Fellowship with others of like minds should be an integral feature of O.T.O. membership, but it is not the most important one. Your own development is the most important part of the experience, and to help you with that, the O.T.O. offers you the personal magical/psycho-dramas of the Degree initiation ceremonies, and exposes you to its supreme secret of magick (and make no mistake about it Brother: it is a blockbuster!) in the form of the Gnostic Mass. These are experiences you must absorb, process, and allow to work their alchemy upon you alone. No matter how many jerks, assholes, or adepts surround you in the O.T.O. and in life, the real work of magick will always be done by *you alone*. You will always be an O.T.O. of *one*.

As you know, there are many Degrees in the O.T.O. but only three Grades. The Highest is that of "Hermit". Hermits *should* be invisible—giving only their inscrutable light to the world.

The next Grade is that of "Lover." Ideally, here is where the sweet mystery of the Holy Grail dominates the magician's meditations and practices. The O.T.O. should be harmonious, fun and beautiful at this level. If it isn't, *you* should be, and you should make it so!

The lowest Grade is "Man of Earth." If I'm not mistaken, this is currently your position in the Order. The highest percentage of O.T.O. members are your Brothers and Sisters at this level. The Man of Earth Grade is peopled with men and women who are still grasping for the meaning of it all—individuals who may or may not be Thelemites in the ideal sense of the word—people who are being tested as to whether or not they currently have what it takes to become Lovers and Hermits. This is something I'm sure you must be asking yourself as well.

No one should be expected to fellowship with people with whom they are uncomfortable. If the members of your local O.T.O. body creep you out or are not the type of people with whom you wish to associate on a regular basis, feel free to study in private (all the good stuff is readily available, lots of it free on the Internet). If you feel it necessary, keep your participation in the local group to a minimum by appearing only when you qualify to take your next Degree and by attending the regular celebration of the Gnostic Mass.

If you don't feel comfortable doing even that, arrange to travel and meet the leaders and members of other bodies around the country or even overseas. I realize this would mean a measure of inconvenience and expense, but it might be worth a try before you throw the O.T.O. baby out with the jerks-and-assholes bathwater.

Finally, consider the possibility the O.T.O. *might not be for you*. Remember:

You don't have to belong to any organization to be a Thelemic magician.

You don't have to be a Thelemic magician in order to gain enlightenment.

You don't have to gain enlightenment in order to be relatively happy in this incarnation.

And you don't have to be relatively happy in this incarnation in order to eventually fulfill your ultimate destiny.

I hope this has been helpful,

Baba Lon

✵

A∴A∴ an Aberration? and Dirty Old Men in the O.T.O.?

[Note: I've left this letter capitalized and punctuated as originally sent. I believe the writer considered it a preferred style.]

Mr. Baba Lon,

i have been working up trying to ask you a few questions for awhile now. i read your book "Understanding the Thoth Tarot" it was a most concise and practical read. i found it elucidating at the time, however i usually (prefer) rather darker formulas, and the more esoteric deep works of Kenneth Grant i liked the stream of consciousness to it, the book itself held a magical charm to it, the way that if you actually read it, it would get under your skin a bit.

i suppose that leads me to my questions, i was inspired to seek out the OTO, because i read of Aleister Crowley's magical exploits and his exploration of the internal realms. i have come to understand that the OTO represents the social order that represents his logos and that it is in truth the A∴A∴ that engaged in the pursuits of higher ritual magick. so my question is does the A∴A∴ even exist anymore? or is the so called "Great Work" merely represent an aberration? it seems like it's almost an exercise in futility. i have talked to a lot of people, i haven't met many who are very serious.

also i wanted to know what your take on what some would call the inherently homo-erotic nature of thelema. 90% of the thelemites i have met are nothing but dirty old men who want to seduce me. i am not going off on tirade, or trying to rail at you about my expectations, i have learned to have none. i am writing this, because i had utilized a lot of esoteric philosophy in personal development and i had seen a dissonance between its letters, and its practice.

according to Regardie in the tree of life magic is the Noble Art, the tradition of Alchemy, i try an incorporate a lot of this into my art work, but i am curious as to whether or not people live by it. if that tradition is alive at all.

Name withheld

....

Dear Name withheld,

My current understanding (this may change at any moment) is that the A∴A∴ is, as it were, an attempt to identify and stratify the spectrum of human consciousness, and as long as consciousness exists there is A∴A∴. The level (or frequency) of consciousness with which you currently identify (as self) is your "Grade" in the A∴A∴.

In essence this has nothing to do with organizations or other individuals. The only person you can ever be sure is living by the traditions of the "Noble Art" is you. As long as you are focused on whether others are living up to your expectations your own work will remain inadequately addressed.

As for the percentage of "dirty old men who want to seduce" you, I think that is despicable and I am sad to hear that has been your experience.

Baba Lon

✷

Gurus and the A∴A∴

Dear Baba Lon,

I've been interested in language, mythology, literature, mathematics, Qabalistic systems, theoretical physics, and a number of other intertwining subjects for quite a few years now, and I have taken a great interest in the general conciliation of the semantic with the syntactical, one might say, through occult "Geisteswissenschaften."* Since I have read and studied a few books by Aleister Crowley (*777, The Book of Thoth,*

---

* *From Wikipedia:* Geisteswissenschaft (more frequently used in plural form Geisteswissenschaften) is a traditional division of faculty in German Universities that included subjects such as Philosophy, History, Philology, social sciences, and sometimes even Theology and Jurisprudence. Most of its subject matter would come under the much larger Humanities faculty in the typical English-speaking University, but it does not contain any arts.

Book 4, etc.) and reached quite a lot of personal views from both mathematical and semantic viewpoints on these matters, since I have had an interest in "the occult" (Eliphas Levi, etc.) for quite some time, and since I have also had an interest in Freemasonry (the works of Albert Pike, Albert Mackay, etc.) and den Illuminatenorden (Weishaupt, but particularly Goethe, etc.), it seems "right," so to say, that I finally join the O.T.O. "officially." This spring I'll be moving to ...., where there happens to be a Lodge.

However, with regard to "the" A∴A∴, you seem to be the only person whom I have encountered in reading who has written anything straightforward and honest about it, who also wrote sensible opinions on the matter of how a student of "Geisteswissenschaften" should be instructed, which were in accord with Hegel's definition, so I must ask you about the A∴A∴

Salome,

Name withheld

....

Hi Name withheld,

I'm a bit of a heretic (at least in the eyes of a few lineage-focused individuals) when it comes to the subject of A∴A∴. Actually, I am more the anarchist.

I'm pretty comfortable with the initiatory world view that uses the Tree of Life to identify major landmarks of human consciousness. The Golden Dawn presented us with the road map; Crowley's A∴A∴ obliges us to take the trip. I believe (at least theoretically) a place can be found on this map for every unit of evolving consciousness. And so, at least from one perspective, I consider every human being a charter member of the big, generic A∴A∴. After all, Crowley considered

Blavatsky an $8^{\circ}=3^{\square}$ Master of the Temple, and I'm almost certain she didn't have any A∴A∴ paperwork from Crowley.

I'm also not uncomfortable with the A∴A∴ program of yoga, meditation, magick and mysticism that Crowley lays out for the student in order for him or her to sequentially master and attain the levels of consciousness associated with the climb up the Tree. Of course I don't think the A∴A∴ program is perfect, nor do I believe it is the only path upward. In fact, it's very clear to me that relatively few spiritual seekers are suited by inclination and temperament for the subtleties and disciplines of A∴A∴ work. Those who are, however, are most often *sublimely* suited.

You might be asking, "If DuQuette is so comfortable with the A∴A∴ in theory and practice, what makes him so heretical?"

The answer is simple. I'm not completely on board when it comes to the A∴ A∴'s student/teacher program, at least how I've been able to observe it in action.

As you know, in the east there is the venerable tradition of the Guru (master) and the Chela (student). This simple system has served to transmit sacred knowledge and disciplines from generation to generation for thousands of years. It works, and it works well. But in order for it to work, the Chela must be driven by something more than zeal to learn, and the Guru must be possessed of something more than mastery of the subject.

The Chela must be able to accept the Guru as God made visible. The Chela must be able to project upon the Master all the qualities of infinite wisdom, omnipotence, and omniscience that one would associate with God. The Guru must be loved as God; believed as God; trusted as God; obeyed as God; served as God.

You might think this is a stupid, naïve, and even dangerous attitude to take towards another human being. But consider for a moment the potential for learning when you believe with all your heart the teacher knows absolutely everything. There is literally nothing you cannot learn at the feet of such a Master.

Of course, the Guru *is* only human and has limits to what he or she can consciously teach. But if the Chela is unaware of those limits, his or her capacity for learning more than the Guru is actually teaching is boundless.

And what does the Guru need to possess to make this arrangement work?

The Guru must possess almost superhuman *restraint*—restraint to not believe his or her own press—restraint not to abuse the Chela's unbounded love and devotion—restraint to reflect the purity of the student's love back upon the Chela—restraint to keep his or her goddamned hands off the attractive Chelas—restraint to keep his or her school, ashram, or movement from turning into a cult. Such restraint is yogic discipline of the highest order—to be worshipped as a living God and not blowing it.

For many reasons that should be obvious, this system does not work particularly well in the west. Not that it couldn't work. It just doesn't; especially when dealing with the spiritual art of Magick. Magicians have teachers, yes. But the magician's God is not one that is easily projected upon another person, especially upon another magician. The magician's career is a bit … lonelier.

Aleister Crowley and his friend, George Cecil Jones, set up a system of magical study and instruction which, on the surface, appears to be a Guru/Chela arrangement. Ideally it is set up so that each student has a superior who is one step more advanced. The superior, in turn, has a superior, who is one step ahead of him or her, etc. Early in my magical career I was eager to join this chain and felt privileged to became the student of Phyllis McMurtry* whose A∴A∴ superior had been Jane Wolfe, whose superior had been Aleister Crowley.

* Later, when Phyllis divorced Grady McMurtry, she resumed the name

Now, as much as I loved and respected Phyllis, it never crossed either of our minds that I should be devoted to her as if she were an omniscient goddess. Nor was it part of the program that I revere the memory of Jane Wolfe or even Crowley to that degree. Obviously the A∴A∴ was meant to be something other than the classic eastern Guru/Chela A∴A∴ system. At least, in my case, I discovered it to be so.

Several years ago I received a letter from a woman who had been teaching magick for many years and had reached a point where her students were now beginning to teach also. She asked my opinion as to what traits a person should look for in a magical teacher. Here's my reply.

What would be the traits of a magical teacher?

Where magical teachers are concerned, I guess I sort of sit with my pea shooter at the very back of the class, and on the extreme left wing of the building.

Of course I've read about great gurus who can read your mind, materialize in your bedroom to correct your spelling; masters who can describe to you your previous incarnations and itemize every article in your karmic baggage. I've read about them—but I've never met one.

Magick, in my opinion, is something that can't be taught. One must learn it. Often you learn it from other people. However, the moment a person starts to identify him- or herself as your teacher (and you as the student), you both are setting yourselves up for disappointment. Oscar Eckenstein, the man Crowley considered to be one of his greatest magick teachers, thought magick was silly and occultists a waste of time. Still, Crowley learned from Eckenstein how to master himself and develop his yogic skills and powers of concentration. Without those skills magick is just theory.

Regardie wasn't my magick teacher, but I learned a lot from his attitudes and the simple example of his life. He answered

---

Seckler, the name of a previous husband.

specific questions when I had them, but nine times out of ten I disagreed with him and ignored his advice (nine out of ten times I was right). I also learned a lot from my formal A∴A∴ Superior, but I must tell you that I learned those lessons in spite of her efforts to educate me rather than because of them. I certainly learned what a horse's ass someone can be when they presume to guide another's magical progress.

But your question is fair and I'm talking like an anarchist. Maybe I should try to make actual suggestions.

The most fundamental advice I can give is to look for somebody who actually has a *life*; someone who can hold his or her own in a room full of people who neither know nor care about magical things; and most importantly, a person who can actually attract lovers from a pool of people who are not at all impressed with his or her mastery of occultism, magick, witchcraft, religion, or politics. Once you've found qualities like that:

Look for somebody who seems to be able to put things in words—things that you already know but didn't know how to say.

Look for somebody who says "I don't know" a lot.

Look for somebody with more questions than answers.

Look for somebody who is relatively happy with his or her life.

Look for somebody who appears to be relatively true to him or herself.

Look for somebody who appears to be actually evolving before your eyes.

Look for somebody who seems to be telling the truth even when it reflects poorly on them.

Look for somebody who would rather study with you than lecture to you.

Finally (and most importantly), look for somebody who will be genuinely happy when you have surpassed him or her intellectually and spiritually.

In other words, look for other students who are studying the same things you are and who may have a bit more experience than you presently have. Don't kid yourself. You said it yourself. Just by remaining on the path you wake up each morning to the inescapable fact that (as little as you know) you already know more than most people about these things. Trust me. One of these mornings you're going to wake up and realize that most, if not all, of the people who know more than you are dead! And there you are—a venerable authority with lots of questions looking for someone to "teach" you the answers. You may as well start looking in the mirror right now.

Well, this probably didn't directly address your A∴A∴ questions. So I'll try to give some "practical" advice and opinions (and please remember my words do not represent the policy of any branch, version, or lineage of A∴A∴). In my personal opinion, if you are thinking about the A∴A∴ you are for all intent and purposes already *in* the A∴A∴ and should feel free to take the *Oath of the Probationer*, sign it, then keep it, burn it, frame it—whatever. Start doing the work as outlined. In a year do the same thing with your Neophyte Oath and paperwork.

If it is important for you to have an objective, *in-the-flesh* formal and classic link, I have no doubt one will eventually appear to sign off on your paperwork. Your work, your challenges and ordeals will be waiting for you ... before your paperwork is signed ... and after.

I hope this has been helpful.

Baba Lon

✳

Be My Mentor?

Dear Baba Lon,

Let me introduce myself. My name is (name withheld). I have acquired the name in honor of the Master of... (presumptuous-sounding magical clan name) ... and the Lord of ... (very serious-sounding dark adjective) ... Magick. I am a budding Thelemite who has found it hard to find a proper mentor to aid me in my studies. Though I have begun my required reading, my progress has been hindered due to the fact that I have no one to direct any questions to. I am not asking you to take on an apprentice. I am simply asking if you would be available to answer some of my future questions to the best of your understanding, as I know that each person interprets the Path differently. If you would find no qualms with this I would be greatly appreciative. If you cannot I will understand.

....

Hi Name withheld,

As I read over my letter (below), I sound really crabby! I'm really not being crabby as I sound, so please, as you read it, apply a jovial lilt to my voice and picture a happy twinkle in my eye!

I'm happy to correspond as much as my time and energy permit. But I hope you understand that my time is limited and I get many requests similar to yours, and that many of the best questions require many hours for me to properly answer. (I'm a slow typist, among other things!)

Furthermore, it seems that many times the people asking the questions could have easily discovered the answers themselves had they done the modicum of homework themselves, or at least spent five minutes on a Google search.

I've concluded that I am never smarter or wiser or well-informed than I am in my published works. I try to write things I would have loved to have read in the early years of my studies. To avoid making me feel like an unpaid reference librarian, I would hope that you have at least done me the courtesy of first reading my books that treat upon the subject of your questions.

Lastly, I must be honest with you. I am a lazy man. I get between fifty and two hundred e-mails each day. When I receive long letters I almost always instantly tag them and I move on. Sometimes I get back to the person and sometimes I do not. Sadly, I must also confess, I never get back to some of the short ones either! I'm out of town (or the country) a good deal of the time, and I've got deadlines for books and articles I've already been paid to write (this is what I do for a living). I teach a weekly class (live) and an online class. And sometimes I just want to sleep, watch TV or get drunk! And sometimes, believe it or not, I actually meditate and engage in magical operations.

Anyway, I hope you take all this in the spirit it is intended, and will feel free to keep in touch.

Baba Lon

✵

Alone in the A∴A∴?

Lon, I have an issue; my focus is not altogether and I need your suggestion on this. Should I use the Student Reading Curriculum of the A∴A∴ or should I go another route? What practice do you suggest I should be doing day in and day out?

I am trying to regroup and get my focus together. Without some kind of step-by-step plan, I feel like I am jumping all over the place. Is this common to people that are new to Thelema?

There is not an O.T.O. near me and the closest one is in .... I am just looking for a little help.

Your friend and Brother,

Name withheld

....

Hi Name withheld,

I honestly don't know you or your situation well enough to confidently advise you. Even if you had an O.T.O. body near you, you would still be dealing with the same issues (minus perhaps a little fellowship and the comfort of knowing that everyone else feels pretty much like you!).

I can only tell you what I did at the beginning of my magical career. I assumed that the A∴A∴ really *was* a true inner plane magical order, and that I was already part of the process. I typed out a copy of the Probationer Oath, read it aloud, signed it, and then burned it. Then I set to work doing the work of the Probationer (as best I could understand it) as outlined in *One Star in Sight* in *Magick in Theory and Practice* and/or in the big blue *Book IV— Magick.** I convinced myself that if I conscientiously did the work my efforts would not escape the attention of the "Secret Chiefs" or whatever the hell you want to call it or them. At the end of one year I did the same thing with the Oath of the Neophyte, and, when I felt ready, the Oath of the Zelator, etc.

---

* Aleister Crowley, et al, *Magick, Liber ABA: Book Four*, ed. Hymenaeus Beta, 2nd rev. ed. (York Beach, ME: Weiser Books, 1997).

At every stage of my development, I've come into contact with the right people and circumstances that have served as the teachers and spiritual links I needed at those precise moments in my magical career. But the real "magical society" I belong to is otherwise completely invisible and profoundly personal. In other words (at least in my case) it is a matter of starting to do the work first and the teachers with further instruction will then come.

Baba Lon

✳

O.T.O. for a Freemason?

Dear Baba Lon,

I am a fellow Freemason and occult student (somewhat uneducated, but serious none the less, ha ha). I know that you are very involved with the O.T.O, and after reading a lot of your work, I've decided that I would direct some questions to you (if you would be so kind as to read them).

I must admit, and I'm sure you understand, in my opinion it's ignorant to just trust anyone who claims to have occult knowledge, and so, it is my opinion (based on your work) that you are someone who can be trusted to converse seriously about these matters.

With that said, here goes:

I am interested in becoming a member of the O.T.O., but as I mentioned I have serious trust issues with anyone claiming to have occult knowledge, so my question is: are the rituals and practices involved truly beneficial as far as obtaining results?

Name withheld

....

Hi Brother Name withheld,

The magick of the O.T.O. is focused pretty narrowly on the dramatic rituals of the Degree Initiations. Like the rituals of Freemasonry, the efficacy of their effect upon and their benefit to the candidate is purely a matter of what the member chooses to do with that experience. The magick of the O.T.O. is that one also finds religious expression in its central public ceremony of the Gnostic Mass (Liber XV). Here too, it is a matter of what each individual chooses to do with the experience.

It's good that you have serious trust issues with anyone claiming to have occult knowledge. Other than the organizational hierarchy (which is routine business, not magick per se), there is nothing resembling a classic student/teacher relationship in the O.T.O. Unless your questions have something to do with the "plot" or the tokens or signs of recognition of a degree you have not yet taken, there is no proprietary or degree-sensitive "knowledge" or teaching. If anyone in the organization presumes to have occult knowledge they do so either because they are deluded or because they do indeed have occult knowledge. Like in all other areas of your life, it will be up to you to spot the phonies or adepts.

The O.T.O. (or any organization or individual) cannot project enlightenment on you. In the O.T.O. nobody reads your diaries, and nobody presumes to judge the level of your attainment. Like Freemasonry, you might find a certain degree of fellowship and an opportunity to meet people with whom you have a great deal in common. Then again, you might not. You might find jerks and assholes in the O.T.O. Then again, you might sometimes be a jerk or an asshole yourself.

Success in the rituals and practices of the O.T.O. is 100 percent dependent upon what you bring to the table.

I hope this has been helpful.

Baba Lon

P.S. I'm sure you've read it before, but just in case, here is the O.T.O.'s Mission Statement:

> Ordo Templi Orientis U.S.A. is the U.S. Grand Lodge (National Section) of Ordo Templi Orientis, a hierarchical, religious membership organization. Our mission is to effect and promote the doctrines and practices of the philosophical and religious

system known as Thelema, with particular emphasis on cultivating the ideals of individual liberty, self-discipline, self-knowledge, and universal brotherhood. To this end, we conduct sacramental and initiatory rites, offer guidance and instruction to our members, organize social events, and engage in educational and community service activities at locations throughout the United States.

✵

Sex Magick in the O.T.O.

Dear Baba Lon,

I made plans a few days ago to visit .... Lodge in .... during my vacation there. This will be my first visit to an O.T.O. lodge and I'm very excited. I have to be completely honest though, because there is one thing that troubles me. Is there somewhere (books, online, etc.) that I can learn more about how the O.T.O. feels about Sex Magick? I don't know anything about it, and I've read statements (by very unreliable sources, believe me) that Sex Magick sometimes plays a role in O.T.O. membership. I'm simply not comfortable with the idea, and would like to know more about the O.T.O.'s stance before I choose to apply for membership. I'm terribly sorry if this sounds immature of me, but my discomfort really is the only thing that has ever kept me from applying. Well, that, and location. The nearest O.T.O. lodge is still four-and-a-half hours away from where I currently am. If you can't answer any of these questions, I completely understand and won't be offended, but I figured I would give it a shot anyway.

I hope I'm not being offensive here. I pray this inquiry won't reflect on what I consider to be a new friendship between you and me. The O.T.O. is very attractive to me, and I would simply like to dispel any ill feelings before seeking membership. Thanks again.

Sincerely,

Name withheld

....

Hi Name withheld,

Please don't feel at all self-conscious. This is a good question and one that is asked many times. I worried in the days and hours before my initiation into the O.T.O. that I was going to be raped and eaten by saggy-titted old Crowley cultists. I was pleasantly disabused.

First of all I want you to know that part of the reason the O.T.O. exists is to prepare her members to discover a great magical secret. Crowley was so impressed with the theory and technique of this secret that once he grasped its power and potential around 1910 he dedicated the rest of his life to practicing and developing it. The secret *is* a Sex Magick technique, and understanding and mastering it is an important part of the Order's work in the highest degrees.

However (and this is a *big* however—one that disappoints a lot of people who were hoping for free love in a sex cult) there is nothing in the O.T.O. system of official degree initiations or practices which would oblige (or even suggest the opportunity for) the candidate or member to engage in an overtly sexual act (or for that matter any act that would be construed by the candidate or member to be against his or her will).

Even though the O.T.O. is the custodian of a magical secret that, at one level, is of a sexual nature, any application or practice of that technique on the part of its members must take place on a purely private and personal basis and completely outside the official knowledge or scrutiny of the Order, its officers or members.

In other words, the sex life of an O.T.O. member is and remains entirely a personal matter.

Try to keep in mind that the O.T.O. is first and foremost a Thelemic Order. The prime directive is, "There is no law beyond *Do what thou wilt*." It would violate the prime directive if the Order were to suggest a person do *anything* against his or her will.

Very few living people can say this, but I'm proud to say I've taken and given every O.T.O. Degree from beginning to end, and not even one of them asked me to ignore the prime directive or in any way threatened to put a dent in my forty-three year monogamist's heterosexual lifestyle. (Not that one has to be a monogamist or heterosexual ... but I think you get the picture.)

Hope this has been helpful.

My best,

Baba Lon

✷

Monogomy and Sexual Ethics in the O.T.O.

Dear Baba Lon,

I have a question for you about sexual ethics based in the order, I saw that you and Soror DuQuette were a couple and in the order together. My question is about this: When I joined a body a few years ago I fell in love with a man. We were happy together until the rest of the people in the group tried using sexual predatory actions and behavior to cause problems in our private relationship. I was just wondering what you do to stop people like this from coming between you two as a couple.

Thank you,

Name withheld

....

Dear Name withheld,

Let me begin by reminding you that the prime directive of Thelema is: "*There is no law beyond Do what thou wilt.*" If it is your will to be monogamous, and it is your partner's will to be monogamous, than that's that! If your lodge members are too ignorant or intolerant to accept that fact and have a civilized relationship with monogamous couples then, in my opinion, they do not have a clue as to what Thelema is all about and you should tell them to "fuck off" and go find a nice sex cult somewhere.

On the other hand, if either or both of you are so insecure in your relationship that you don't know for sure whether or not it is your will to be monogamous, it's not only your lodge brethren who threaten your relationship—indeed, every man, woman and child on the planet becomes for you a potential sexual predator .

Call me unmagical and unpatriotic if you want, but I believe it is more important to be happy with your domestic life than it is to lead or be part of an O.T.O. body or any organization. We have lots of O.T.O. friends with whom (under different circumstances) I'm sure we could happily enjoy more intimate relations. But over the years we've learned that for us (in our particular life circumstances) the negatives of such relationships would simply outweigh the positives of the stable home life we feel is necessary for us to pursue undistracted our Great Work. We are probably in the minority here, but so what!

Sex, not promiscuity, is a big part of magick. Promiscuity can be fine (wonderful, in fact) under certain circumstances. It's even fun to have promiscuous friends if they understand and respect where you're coming from. But please don't confuse promiscuity with Sex Magick, and certainly don't confuse it with Thelema.

My best,

Baba Lon

Marriage

And while we're speaking of marriage and monogamy and all that, Baba Lon has for a number of years been legally empowered to marry couples. This is something he really enjoys doing, especially for friends. Once upon a time a young man and young woman came to the home of Baba Lon and St. Constance and said something like:

"Baba Lon, we are in love and have come to ask you to marry us. But even in our joy we have fears. All around us we see the sadness and strife of unhappy couples. Most marriages today end in bitter divorce. The newspapers are filled with terrible tales of jealous lovers who beat and kill one another. We read that more pregnant women are murdered by the fathers of their children than die by any other cause. These atrocities, committed in the name of love, make us reticent to take the marriage vows.

"Baba Lon, you and St. Constance have been married for many earth-years. We observe you to be happy. You make each other laugh. You touch and hug and speak with joy about your son. What is the secret of your love? What wisdom can you share with us at the beginning of our journey together? What must we do to be as happy as Baba Lon and St. Constance?"

Baba Lon adjusted his turban and looked to St. Constance as if silently asking permission to speak. Eventually he cleared his throat and said, "My friends, I must tell you that you will never make one another happy."

He then reached for his guitar and (as everyone feared) he began to sing:

Love Is Bigger Than Happiness

So you're in love, and want to wed,
  But see most marriages end up dead.
To Baba Lon you've voiced your fears.
  Yes! I've been married forty-three* years.

St. Constance is the perfect wife,
  Brings love and beauty to my life.
As husbands go, I'm not so bad,
  And we've both done well as Mom and Dad.

Our marriage endures for years and years,
  Through ups and downs and fits and tears,
Because we've learned, and now confess,
  Love is bigger than happiness.

Vital to life as happiness is,
  Hers must be hers and his must be his.
The old cliché is worn and sappy,
  But only *you* can make you happy.

---

* This was written in 2010.

So I say to the would-be mated,
Communication is over-rated.
Probe not too deep each other's head.
Contempt is born when mystery's dead.

Monogamy's not for everyone.
It has its pros. It has its cons.
But once you've pledged to that relation,
Try to be good at it … for the duration.

Be not too quick to throw in the towel.
Don't stray, don't cruise, don't sneak, don't prowl.
Chances are good if you're miserable here
In no time at all you'd be miserable there.

So remember my words through the pain and stress
Love is bigger than happiness.
I bless you both and wish you luck,
I'll marry you now for a hundred bucks.

A few years back I had the honor of officiating at the wedding ceremony for our son, Jean-Paul, and his lovely bride, Miwa. I happily imparted to them the secret that I believe is the key to a long and relatively happy marriage … at least what has worked for Constance and me.

The Secret of Marriage

When two strong souls, and two strong wills
And two strong minds unite,
There will come rounds when standing your grounds
Will turn into a fight.

So here and now, before reciting your vows,
And while you're high as a kite,

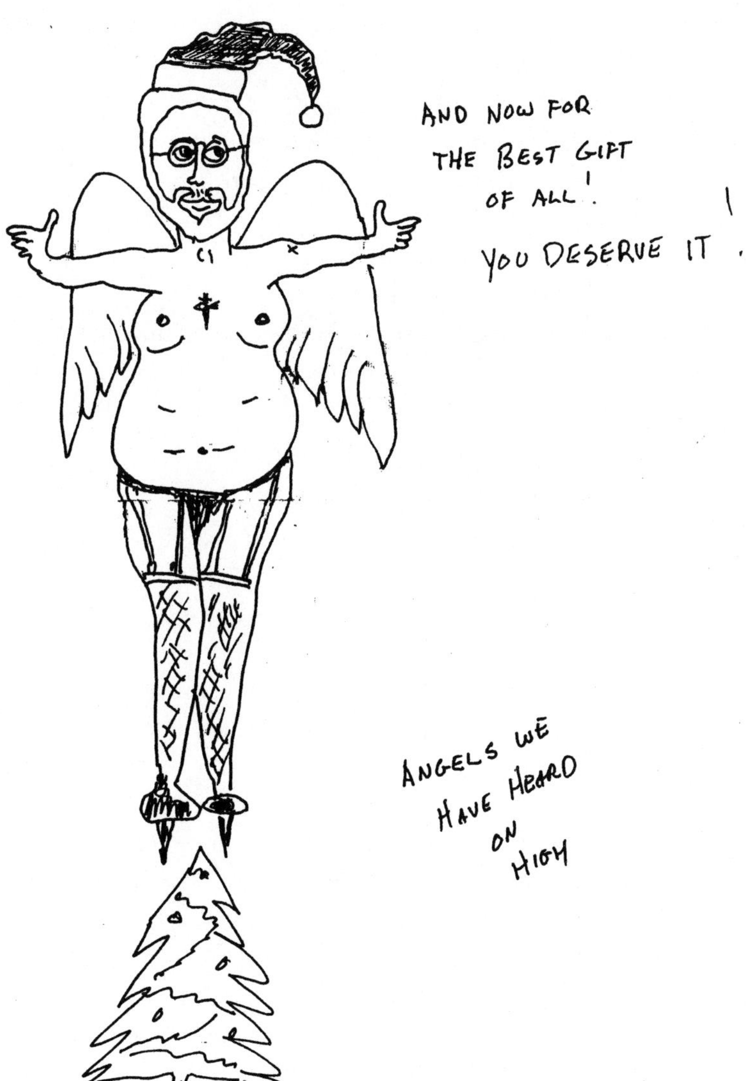
AND NOW FOR
THE BEST GIFT
OF ALL!
YOU DESERVE IT!
ANGELS WE
HAVE HEARD
ON
HIGH

Agree that one of you will *know everything*,
And the other will *always be right*.

This compromise is very wise.
You'll need it day and night.
It's an understanding that's not demanding.
It's unbreakable, try as you might.

So leave behind the undefined.
Step boldly into the light
Of a world where *one of you* knows everything,
And the *other* is always right.

✺

Thelema and Politics

My father, Abba Baba Lon, told me never to discuss religion or politics in a bar. As I grow older his words take on greater dimensions of wisdom. It's a real pity though. There are few things I like more than discussing religion and politics … especially when I'm drinking.

For over half my life I have been involved in the magical and administrative adventures of Ordo Templi Orientis. The O.T.O. is a magical society founded around 1900 that embraces the "Law of Thelema," a philosophical (some say, "religious") concept based on a "received" text, *Liber AL vel Legis*, a.k.a. *The Book of the Law*.

The Book of the Law is unique among holy books because it forbids anyone to interpret it for another. This, in my opinion, is a good thing because many passages, if taken (or mistaken) literally, can be very unsettling. (I burned my first copy the moment I was through reading it.)

Obviously I came to terms with my irrational fears, for I am currently the O.T.O.'s U.S. Deputy Grand Master, and Archbishop of its ecclesiastical arm, Ecclesia Gnostica Catholica. As such, I get letters. Some of the letters, like the ones to follow, concern statements in the text of *The Book of the Law* which, if projected on a political canvas, would suggest some very disturbing things. Couple that with the reputation of the book's scribe and we have a recipe for freak-out.

As you will soon see I come out of the political closet and confess to and attempt to justify my political attitudes. I hope the reader who finds him or herself on the other end of the political spectrum will not think too unkindly of me.

✳

Can a Thelemite Be a Liberal?

Dear Baba Lon:

I have been studying books on the "western esoteric tradition" for a couple of years, and have developed a particular appreciation for Aleister Crowley's works and ideas, with one exception: his sociopolitical views. I am a liberal humanist, and I oppose "social Darwinism," or the view "let the strong survive and thrive, and stamp down the weak and helpless" with all my heart. Crowley advocates this view, including in *Liber AL vel Legis*, which is put forth as "holy writ which is not to be changed." Even most conservatives in America insist that they are not "social Darwinists." In other words, Crowley is to the right of Attila the Hun. Are the rest of us excluded from being Thelemites (for example, are we barred from initiation in the O.T.O.)? I ask this sincerely, since all the rest of Crowley's work is so excellent, and with this single exception, I am whole-heartedly drawn to Thelema.

Sincerely,

Name withheld

....

Dear Name withheld,

Yes name withheld. A liberal can be a Thelemite. (Sounds a bit like "Yes Virginia. There is a Santa Claus.")

I consider myself a liberal humanist. Actually, I'm a radical liberal humanist. I guess the polite term in today's American politics is "progressive." So is Constance, and so are most of our closest friends in and out of the O.T.O. I can't speak for them, but my motives are entirely selfish. It's simply that I have come to the conclusion it is in my best interest to live in a stable environment undisturbed and unencumbered by violent social unrest. Being surrounded, distracted, and menaced by hungry, unhappy, unhealthy, out-of-work, homeless, downtrodden, fellow citizens is *not* conducive to my efforts to quietly pursue my spiritual Great Work.

I would venture to guess if we were to poll the 3,000 + members of the Order in the world (something which would never happen) we would most likely discover at least a respectable percentage of members who would probably consider themselves liberal humanists or something like that. The majority of those remaining would probably consider themselves Libertarians, Independents, or Anarchists. We even count as dear Brothers in Thelema an outrageously entertaining and provocative right-wing radio talk show host, and possibly the next Republican Lieutenant Governor of a state I'll leave unnamed.

That being said, in the O.T.O. and ultimately in Thelema, one's politics is entirely a personal matter. It has to be. In my opinion there can't be a Thelemic political party unless it was one that told its party members to vote for whomever they personally preferred and support the programs they personally agree with. Anything less would be like saying, "We believe that 'there is no law beyond *Do What Thou Wilt*' and we want a law to make you believe that too!"

Of course, it is likely that many individuals who embrace Thelema's philosophy of personal liberty would want to live in an environment that allows them and all others this freedom. Naturally, many of us tend to support measures, candidates, and parties that promise strong civil liberties and such. But the source of these attitudes are most often not dictated by the tenets of Thelema per se, but from ideals of *youthful idealism,* or our *intelligent observation,* or our *mature common sense*, or simply our sense of *human decency.*

It is possible (owing to infinite and unknown factors of karma or personal issues) that a person might need to spend a season or a lifetime as a social Darwinist, or a Nazi or another such creature in order to "do" his or her will in this incarnation. It is not for any of us to judge *on that level.*

I admire Crowley too. He's my holy prophet. But I'm not obliged to comb my hair, or select my wardrobe, or my diet, or my lovers, or vote the way he did. Thelema is bigger than Aleister Crowley. And nobody can tell you how to interpret *The Book of the Law.* If anyone ever does you should feel empowered to give them a hearty "fuck you!"

I hope this has been helpful.

Baba Lon

....

Dear Baba Lon,

Hello, and thank you for your response. However, in reading your response to my question I realized that I didn't ask my question clearly or precisely enough. So if you'll bear with me, I'll try to ask it again.

The O.T.O website states: "If you decide to pursue full membership as a 1st degree, you will be stating that you accept *The Book of the Law* as written, without wishing to change it."

I am sure you will recognize the following as quotations from *The Book of the Law:*

... the kings of the earth shall be kings forever. The slaves shall serve.

Stamp down the wretched and the weak: this is the law of the strong: this is our law and the joy of the world.

Mercy be let off: damn them who pity! Kill and torture: spare not: be upon them!

We are not for the poor and sad: the lords of the earth are our kinfolk.

Ye are against the people, O my chosen!

Pity not the fallen! I never knew them. I am not for them. I console not: I hate the consoled and the consoler.

If many O.T.O. members are "progressive or liberal humanists," how did they bring themselves to "accept" such quotes as the above? A human society run along such lines would be hell on earth.

Since Reagan was elected, our own country has moved in that direction, it has become just that for many people: "Every man for himself and let the devil take the hindmost." I thought we "progressives" were opposed to having human society operate according to the law of the jungle. And how can the above quotes be squared with the O.T.O.'s repeated proclamations, in their literature and on their website, of "brotherhood" as something the organization advocates? I mean no offense—I'm sincerely puzzled. I've found Crowley's ideas on practically every *other* subject to be so outstanding that I was starting to dream of becoming an O.T.O. member.

Yours truly,
Name withheld

....

Hi again,

The answer (for me at least) is very simple. I consider and meditate upon such passages as metaphors concerning the nature of my own being, my own struggles, my own flaws and aspirations. If I take it beyond that, it ceases to be a holy book and becomes no better than the Bible or the Koran. For me, the projection of "scriptural" passage upon the world of politics is a major cause for most of the world's ills. My god! I'm a vegetarian too. Do you think I actually think that *The Book of the Law* is telling *me* to eat human flesh or sacrifice cattle and children?

Of course there will always be "people" who are stupid enough to do such things. I'm happy to say I'm *against* those "people."

"Accepting" *The Book of the Law* without wishing to make changes in it does not suggest that you are accepting Crowley's or anyone's interpretation of what it means. It does suggest that you are willing to search for truth everywhere, even in a book that you may never understand and which might scare the shit out of you. I can't tell you or anyone else how to interpret *The Book of the Law*, and I certainly will not burden anyone with my moment-by-moment interpretations. But, with all due respect, I believe you are missing a very big point here. I certainly wouldn't look to *Liber AL*, or the Bible, the Torah, the Koran, the Tao Teh King, the Book of Mormon, or any sacred scripture as a political manifesto. Yikes!

From a magical (or even Zen) perspective an idea is only true in so much as it contains within itself its own opposite. Not everyone resonates to the idea of finding the light even in the darkness. *The Book of the Law* certainly does a good job of initially turning off those who do not grasp this age-old and fundamental concept ... and perhaps it needs to.

I just thank the gods that when Election Day rolls around your vote and my vote probably won't cancel each other out!

My best,

Baba Lon

Angels & Demons

✷

Are Angels Real?

Hello Baba Lon,

Enochian Magick ... this is about "making contact" with "things," yes? I mean, that was the "point" of Dee's and Kelly's work, was it not?

I read in Crowley's *Enochian Sex Magick* (nice title by the way) that you envision things by closing your eyes. I believe you were talking about evoking one of the angels ... some entity that was silvery-mercury-like...

This always struck me as ... well, kinda scary, and a little abstract. I close my eyes and see a being "in my mind" in front of me? Too close for comfort, I would imagine.

I've heard of using a "mirror" or "keek-stane" (Buckland), and even externally using a triangle ... I've even seen a house-fly ... but I've never seen an elephant fly ... sorry.

Here's the question. Are these entities "real"?

Let me go in this direction: Crowley, in his "early" years, has some passage in the Goetia, with Mathers, I believe, that states something along the lines of "these beings may just be part of your normal psyche, but they are treated as external." (My books are upstairs in the library, and I'm tired and lazy right now; add that to my horrible ability to recite quotes).

I've been flipping through *Magick Without Tears* lately, and this was written by an "older Crowley"—so the intro says (and the dates seem to agree). There are parts in this book that seem to lend credence to "actual," "separate," "sentient," "macrocosmic" or "microcosmic" entities with which one is strongly recommended to communicate.

So ... my dear sir, if I can call you "my dear sir"... what the heck? I mean, what is your position on this matter?

I know from a certain perspective, one could argue the collective-unconsciousness ... or collective-subconciousness...

And, before you go all mystic on me, remember I've been reading *Magick Without Tears*, and that has enough of this kind of double-speak that makes me fall in love with Crowley all over again, but it pisses me off at the same time.

Do you have anything you'd like to say? Maybe I should just sit here, and eventually, I'll either become nothing, or everything ... good luck and goodbye.

Name withheld

....

Dear Name withheld,

Are these entities "real"? Can they knock over a lamp?

No.

But they can frighten you so much (or fill you with so much ecstasy, or make you laugh so hard, or make you see wonders beyond your imagination, or shock you with embarrassing insight about yourself, or otherwise startle you out of the sleepy dream world you think is reality) that you piss your pants, jump up and knock over a lamp!

Baba Lon

✳

Commanding the Archangels

Dear Baba Lon,

I'll try to keep this brief as I can, but there are two issues I would like your opinion on.

First I have already talked to the previous lodge master of the O.T.O. Lodge here in town.

Before I moved out here I had regular, conscious out-of-body experiences (OBEs) at will. Once I moved here they stopped except for a few uncontrolled ones. The Lodge Master told me he thought it might have something to do with the increased solar energy I was being exposed to. Truth is I was even having trouble opening/activating my chakras to previous levels that I was accustomed to. All of a sudden within the past nine months my OBEs have started up again, but still uncontrolled, with little memory recall. I have noticed a sharp pain along with the usual vibrations located below my navel that I have not experienced before. I believe it's not a good sign. I have never felt pain when activating a chakra center, just a vibration that spreads throughout my body. I am not sure what to do about it.

Second, I am familiar with a story of your first goetic experience and empathize with the situation you were in when you did it. I myself have a family I support working full-time and I'm trying to get my degree to get a promotion, and money is always an issue.

When I tried goetic evocation of the same spirit you wrote about in your first experience, I could not get him to appear visibly; although there was a smoky-something present, it was not contained within my triangle of art but kinda zipped around the room like it was trying to avoid me directly looking at it. There was no communication between us that I could recognize. So the ritual must have failed, which would mean one or more things in my ritual was wrong. How do I know what it is?

And why is it that I can see the angels in my mind's eye in the Lesser Banishing Ritual of the Pentagram (LBRP) present but they don't really take commands? (By the way, the vibration of the divine names looks like a prayer, *i.e.*, YHVH, Adonai, Eheieh, AGLA looks like YHVH, lord who is what it is, etc. Is that why the God doesn't come in that ritual like it says in the book?)

And finally, I should be able to use the Greater Ritual of the Pentagram to evoke elementals, not just their qualities; but I don't feel, see, or sense a presence. Could you tell me why or how to fix that?

Out of all the practice I have been doing I know that my brain is interpreting things differently. I feel like my aura is stronger and things that didn't make sense when reading them before do make sense now. But when I try to allow myself a serious working, (one like Crowley suggests is doable) it just doesn't seem to come together.

I apologize this was longer than I had originally planned it to be. But if I could get your thoughts/opinions on what I have written that would be great, and don't worry about writing something that would offend me. I am good with criticism.

Thanks again for your time,

Name withheld

....

Hi Name withheld,

I really don't know what to tell you about your OBEs except that I also go through seasons when I can pop out easily and seasons when I can't. I don't think your exposure to "solar energy" has much to do with it. (I consistently project in my half-sleep after I gorge on my wife's broccoli quiche [no kidding]!) I'm also not sure what to tell you about your chakra pains. Don't dismiss the possibility that it might be purely physical. If it continues, see your doctor. I am given to understand that the various psychic (chakra) centers can act as exit points when astrally projecting. Indeed, many of my nocturnal involuntary excursions seem to be characterized by an intense thrill sensation in my solar plexus region. I've also experienced severe pain in the medulla area of my brain stem during unpleasant or confusing OBEs. This leads me to at least consider the possibility that I "exit" my physical body through different chakras.

Don't worry about not "seeing" angels, spirits, elementals, etc. Proceed as if you did. (If you could hear them talking to each other they might be saying something like, "Don't move. He can't see us so he doesn't believe we're here. I hope he doesn't write DuQuette.") Proceed to work without "seeing" them and focus on the effects of your working.

As for as "commanding" the archangels in the Lesser Banishing Ritual of the Pentagram—where the fuck in the LBRP does it say anything about "commanding" the archangels to do anything? They "come" when called because they are already there! (The same thing goes for God.) Face east and everything in the universe that's in front of you is Raphael. Where an archangel is concerned, it is *you* who needs to impress *him* by showing him you recognize his position in the magical universe. Command him? Command him to do what? Bring you money? Get you a girlfriend? Harm an enemy? Those are chores for beasties dramatically lower on the spirit totem pole. With all due respect, you have to get straight what you're trying to do in these rituals, and what the hierarchy of spirits is really all about.

Just keep plugging away and try not to over think things. After all, this is a spiritual science. Whenever you think you haven't made any magical progress, just ask yourself, "Where was I a year ago; two years ago? Was I more magical then?" I can almost guarantee your answer will always be "No."

My best,

Baba Lon

✵

I Am the Angel Sariel

Dear Baba Lon,

I purchased your book *Enochian Vision Magick* only a few days ago. I must say that it is of great interest to me, and I have really enjoyed reading it. I respect you not only as an author, but as what I believe to be a great teacher and well learned individual.

I've been seriously confused recently as to my own connection to the book of Enoch. My heart and soul say everything I know to be true about angels is absolutely correct; and yet, my head gets in the way. The "elemental" world around me seems to swear that my gut instincts are wrong. I may as well just come out and say it: I believe my soul's origins are that of the angel Sariel.

I know I have many gifts to share with the world, and it seems as though so much of the world is in desperate need of change; however true this is, I have a strong hesitation to be open about this. I spoke with an angel therapy practitioner last year who explained that, in past lives, I have been persecuted for my beliefs, and that I will be persecuted again. I honestly dislike using the word "beliefs," especially when I am speaking of things I know to be true and have nothing to do with believing. This is not a new revelation; I have seen, heard, and felt things since childhood. I've always been incredibly sensitive to receiving divine information and yet not always tuned into the wavelength, so-to-speak. A lot of the time it sounds like radio static with the occasional word or two from a station before the channel is changed.

I feel jumbled. I must admit, I am very nervous about sending this e-mail and how it will be received. Ultimately I think it is for the best to send it. I realize you must be a very busy person, but I do hope that you will find time to write back to me. I look to you, as a wise-one and teacher, for assurance of what is real in a world that tells me everything is fake.

Name withheld

....

Hi Name withheld,

I would like to be able to give you "... assurance of what is real in a world that tells (you) everything is fake," but ultimately I am in no better position than you to do that. I have a feeling that realization of the "real" is the last thing we experience as our consciousness melds and fizzles into godhead...

"Oh! THAT's what's real!"

psssssssssssssssst

Until that final moment of realization, all the "reals" are just as phony as the fakes. So why worry about it?

You are a being of consciousness whether your consciousness currently views itself as an archangel or a toad. If you "are" or have been "sent by" Sariel, then get on with the business of being your Sariel-self. Start by setting to work to understand the "self" you now inhabit; after all, it is the 'self' chosen to be the vessel of whomever you are.

Your quest—your duty—your destiny is as close as the everyday *you*. You'll find far more wisdom *there* than you will from angel therapy practitioners or cynical, gray-haired magicians like me.

I imagine that this probably has not been helpful, but it is about all the "wisdom" I can muster this morning.

I wish you the best of luck with your life and your quest.

My best,

Baba Lon

✸

How Do I Redeem a Demon?

Dear Baba Lon,

Please excuse me if this letter is written somewhat awkwardly. English is not my first language. I am currently studying with much interest the book you and Dr. Hyatt wrote, *Aleister Crowley's Illustrated Goetia,** and I have several very fundamental questions that I hope you will find the time to answer.

You refer repeatedly to the sigil or seal of the spirit being "charged." What exactly charges this object? Is it the ceremony? How can I be sure the seal has been charged? Is the charge permanent? Does it ever wear off? What do I do if I want to change the instructions I give the spirit? What happens if I lose or misplace a charged seal? Can I store the spirit's seal in the brass bottle? If not, what exactly is the brass bottle for?

Most importantly, how do I share my good fortune and spiritual success with a spirit? Isn't that a bit like making a

---

* Aleister Crowley, Lon Milo DuQuette, Christopher S. Hayat, David P. Wilson. *Aleister Crowley's Illustrated Goetia*. (Scottsdale, AZ: New Falcon Publications, 1992. 2nd rev. ed. 2000, 3rd rev. and expanded ed. 2010).

deal with the spirit, which is something I believe you advise strongly against?

Name withheld

....

Dear Name withheld,

You ask very good questions, and I will do my best to answer them. Let me begin by assuring you that the best source of answers to these questions, and indeed any questions of a magical or spiritual nature, lies within yourself. Magick is an art and magicians are artists. Picasso and Monet could agree or disagree about the advantages of oil points versus water colors or the virtues of different canvases, but one should not expect them to even attempt to understand each other's perception of truth. I will answer the questions you raise, but you must remember the answers are true *only* to the degree that they temporarily represent my understanding the art of goetic evocation. It is entirely up to you as a magician/artist to use, amend, or discard any of this information as your magical career evolves.

Yes, the ceremony of evocation activates (or charges) the seal which has been placed in the Triangle. The energy which executes this activation is the Magician's concentrated Will, which has been sharpened and focused by all the physical and mental preparations of the evocation. The spirit appears* upon the seal, and that "vision" serves to charge the seal by indelibly imprinting on the magician's subconscious mind that image.

* Don't expect to "see" the spirit in exactly the same way you see your next-door neighbor. I know goetic magicians who report extremely vivid phenomena during evocations, but it is more the exception than the rule. Also, I see no evidence suggesting that such phenomena have any bearing on the success or failure of the working.

Years from now you may forget that you ever performed that particular evocation, but your subconscious mind will not forget, and (from one point of view) the subconscious is the natural abode of the spirits of the Goetia. So, yes—in one respect the ceremony activates the seal permanently. To deactivate it you will have to *update* your subconscious mind with the experience of another evocation and another vision. This needs to be done ceremonially with the same care and preparation you expended in the original evocation.

Perhaps you are beginning to see that evocation is a formal, conscious dialog and relationship between your conscious and subconscious mind. The reason you do not wish to lose or forget where you put an activated seal is because you do not wish to lose the lines of communication you so painstakingly established between these "worlds." A goetic spirit, once evoked, is an awakened giant ready to serve you. You do not want to forget there is an awakened giant in the cellar. The reason you take great care to store the seal in a special container is so you will consciously reinforce the relationship. Each time your eyes fall upon the container you are reminded of the evocation—reminded of the spirit, and how that little devil is pledged to your service and well-being. This serves to recharge both you and the spirit. Every time you see or think about the special box containing the spirit's seal, you should feel the same warmth of satisfaction a dog's master feels when he is able to feed his faithful pet a special treat.

Sealing up the spirit's seal in a brass bottle is a form of punishment and should only be resorted to after numerous attempts to form an amicable relationship have failed. It is not the same as destroying the spirit's seal (which is the last option, after which I advise you to never attempt to evoke that particular spirit again), but is intended to demonstrate to the spirit that if it is not willing to help you that you are quite willing to see that it doesn't hurt you while you decide its fate. Pure and simple, it is an intimidation device. Before resorting to sealing it in the brass bottle, however, you can apply a bit of torture by putting its seal in a metal box in the Triangle. Also, in the Triangle should be a bowl of flaming liquid or hot coals. The metal box should have a chain attached to it so that at the proper moment you can (from the safety of the circle) pick up the chain of the box with the point of your sword and suspend it over the fire.

How do you share your good fortune and spiritual success with a spirit? That is an extremely good question, and one that can only be answered by you. I am reminded of the old American cowboy movies where the hero rescues the girl and captures the bank robbers, but only after he has been pulled out of a deadly pool of quicksand by his faithful horse. In the really old movies the cowboy doesn't kiss the *girl* at the end of the film, he kisses his *horse*!

If you can endure yet another one of my old movie analogies, let's look at it this way: you are the captain of a pirate ship and the spirit is the unruly sailor you've trained (or whipped into shape) to be a worthy crew member.

Once it is tamed, trained, and working on your team, you sail together to exotic ports and both become enriched by the adventures and enterprises you lead. Ideally you continue to do great things and continue to grow in knowledge and wisdom and (if you are truly wise) you keep refining the character, skills, and duties of your crew, and the importance and holiness of your enterprises. Finally, when you are truly successful and save the empire, you and your entire crew are presented to the queen and get knighted.

I'm only being half silly here. Every case is different and unique. As you gain enlightenment you keep applying that enlightenment to the character and duties of the spirits you have taken responsibility for. Recognizing a job well done is a private and entirely internalized affair. You give credit where credit is due.

Orobas, the spirit I wrote about in *My Life with the Spirits,* and we have come a long way together; indeed we are part of each other. Just as I feel I have evolved a little bit in the last three decades, so too has my spirit friend. It is a holy relationship.

In my particular magical/spiritual discipline I seek union with a divine counterpart which I call the Holy Guardian Angel. I, by no stretch of the imagination, have yet to achieve what I believe to be complete and perfect communion with this "being," but I have been vouchsafed glimpses and moments of ecstatic wonder when I realize, however briefly, that I am part of an unimaginably greater life. In the nomenclature of Western Hermeticism, these moments are my Holy Guardian Angel attempting to "raise me up."

To a goetic spirit, the magician is the Holy Guardian Angel; and just as there are people in the world who are so base and ignorant that they will end this incarnation without ever having a spiritual thought no matter how hard their Holy Guardian Angels may try to contact them, so too in your magical universe it is likely there are goetic spirits who may not be ready to be calmed down enough to have a relationship with you. You might never be able to work effectively with these particular sprits.

For those with whom you can form a working relationship only you will know how to *share your good fortune and spiritual success.*

I wish you the best of luck with your magical career.

Sincerely,

Baba Lon

Where the Hell Did I Go Wrong?

Dear Baba Lon,

I am having a little problem and I hope you can give me some advice as to how to correct the situation. My problem has to do with the Goetia[*] and summoning the spirit Andromalius. In your book *Tarot of Ceremonial Magick*[†] it says:

"He is an Earl, Great and Mighty, appearing in the form of a man holding a great serpent in his hand. His office is to bring back both a thief, and the goods which be stolen; and to discover all wickedness, and underhand dealing; and to punish all thieves and other wicked people and also to discover treasures that be hid …"

The situation is this: I have been trying to get in contact with Andromalius because it is said that he returns lost items to the original owners, among many other things. In my situation, a great deal of money has been taken from me and I want back what I had initially invested. I've already tried contacting Andromalius three times.

The first time I had gotten in touch with some spirit that came in the form of a white dog, a big snake and a white rabbit. He didn't leave when I gave him the license to depart until I yelled at him (using the names of God) and he left, but first agreed to show me a sign to let me know he was working for me. This was out in the woods by the way.

* *The Goetia: The Lesser Key of Solomon the King: Clavicula Salomonis Regis, Book One.* Translated by Samuel Liddell MacGregor Mathers: edited, annotated and introduced with additions by Aleister Crowley: Illustrated Second Edition with new annotations by Aleister Crowley: Edited by Hymenaeus Beta (York Beach, ME: Weiser Books, 1995).

† Lon Milo DuQuette, *Tarot of Ceremonial Magick* (York Beach, ME: Samuel Weiser, 1995), p. 219

The second time was in my room where I had created the Circle and Triangle. I received what I had thought to be him promising a sign but to no avail.

The third time, which was two nights ago, I was in the same, taped circle and did all my conjurations mentally. And after focusing a while on his sigil, a black-eyed, horned, goat-footed imp appeared in the triangle, saying that it was Andromalius. He told me that he hopes that I will make an offering to him, and that it better be something more than MacDonald's. He asked me to help destroy a common enemy. When I asked who, he gave out a name (which I do not remember). I declined to help.

So then he asked me to speak of my desire. But before I could give him my original charge, he tried to leave the triangle and come into my Circle. I commanded him back in the Triangle. I gave him the charge as to what I want. He agreed, but when I gave him the license to depart, he walked over to my printer and said he could fix it as a sign that he was working for me. (Earlier that day, my printer had jammed up and I couldn't fix it.) So, thinking that it was a good idea, I agreed, and then commanded him back into the triangle where he complained to me that the triangle was too small for him. He whined like a little kid complaining about his parent's command.

I told him the next time I would make the triangle bigger and he went back in. I then gave him a second charge. (I had two charges for him but thought that it would be best to charge him once to test him out; but since he volunteered to fix my printer, I thought it would be best to get the two charges out of the way.)

After stating what I wanted done and telling him what I would give him as an offering in return (a beautiful picture with his sigil on it and engraving his sigil in precious metal with some of the money that was returned to me in full). I warned him that if he didn't do what I had asked, I was going to summon him up again and burn his sigil to completely banish him, and had asked if he understood and he said, "Yes, Master" in a sneering, cunning sort of way.

I gave him the license to depart and he said that he was too tired to do anything now, but tomorrow he would show me a sign, and he walked out of the building's wall. Now when I went to bed, the image of this ugly imp came into my head and said that he was not a rag doll to be played with and he will hold up his end, but I should make sure I hold up mine.

I told him that I wasn't playing with him nor would I summon him to deceive him, and that I was hopeful to see his sign to let me know that he will do what I ask. Needless to say, the next day nothing happened, but I was cool about it because I had summoned him after 12:00 a.m. and when he said the next day, he could have meant Sunday (which is today).

Well, I fixed the damn printer on my own (hurray) and still no sign of him at all. I am willing to try to summon him again but this time I want to get the real Andromalius.

Now I am asking you in your opinion, is Andromalius the one that I really need to return something to me or should I try another? This time however, I am going to give only one charge and only the one that is most important to me.

Where the hell did I go wrong? I have been reading your book over and over again but I feel that I did not miss anything. So what can I do (to the best of my ability) to make sure this time around I get Andromalius? I appreciate your time in reading this and I hope (pray actually) that you can help me out A.S.A.P. Until then, I am holding off my fourth and possibly final evocation.

Respectfully yours,

Name withheld

....

Dear Name withheld,

Without going into unnecessary detail with you concerning your workings, I'll just share one little tidbit that might enable you to answer your own questions in this matter. Please don't think me rude if I'm late or completely remiss in answering follow-up questions.

It looks like at the moment you're missing the big picture on what kind of magick you're trying to work. First of all, you'll save yourself a lot of confusion and frustration if you start out by remembering that in Goetia you need to treat the spirit as if it were the *source of your problem* (because it is!). You don't make fucking *deals* with the source of your problem! One of you, either you or the demon, must become a groveling slave and it had better not be you!

The magician is the boss! Always! The magician makes the demands! Not the demon. Can't you see? For your entire life (up until the moment of the evocation) the spirit has been screwing with you—bargaining with you—making you weak—making you confused—making you the type of person these problems torment. And it'll continue to screw with you until you stop making deals with the little bastard. That evocation was your first opportunity to say, "It's time for you to shut up for a change and do what I say!"

My God man! Don't promise it anything—hamburgers, pizza, blood, bats, cats, bugs, semen, spit, buggers, flowers, seeds, dirt, rocks, poop—nothing! It doesn't make demands on or suggestions to *you.* You make demands on *it.* If you succumb to any of the demands of the spirit you're not performing Goetia, you're performing "anti-Goetia" and the spirit will end up writing in *its* magical diary how successfully it evoked *you*!

Of course it will try to make demands and dictate conditions. Can't you see? It's been doing that your whole life. Don't listen to it anymore. Learn to say "No!" Know what you want and stick to it. If it asks for *anything* get pissed. Tell it, "Fuck you! I'm the one making demands here! Shut up and listen!" Make it afraid of *you*! That's the key! You don't need it if it continues to work against you. Let it know that if it doesn't play ball, you will blast it from existence and mean it.

Most importantly, before even beginning an operation like this, think about what your problem *really* is. Do you want a *specific little* thing to happen in a *specific little* way or do you want your life to get better? If the answer is the latter, think about asking the spirit to do something about *that*.

Don't try to micromanage how the spirit should go about fulfilling the charge. Tell it to work without harming you, your loved ones or the fragile ecosystem; but other than that let it work in its own way.

One more thing (and this might be the most important part of our conversation). Andromalius brings back things that are *stolen*. You characterize your loss as being an "investment." Investments suggest an element of risk, which the investor is prepared to take for the chance of profit. The investment game is: the higher the chance of making a profit, the higher the risk. If you, even in the back of your mind, look at this as an investment loss, Andromalius is not your guy. Unless the situation is one in which something has been taken from you unexpectedly and against your will and with no hope of return or reward, then I suggest in the strongest terms that you reconsider enlisting the aid of Andromalius, or any other goetic spirit for this particular matter.

Anyway, be fearless; use your common sense and your sense of humor. Lose that and you're lost! Good luck!

Baba Lon

✷

I Want to Use Demon Sigils at the Office

Hi Baba Lon!

I know you are super-busy, but if you have the time to answer my question I would be so grateful.

We have some people who work closely with us whom we found to be conspiring against us.

I am wondering if there is any safe way (like posting a sigil over the office door or something) that could just boomerang their efforts away from us?

I really appreciate your time.

Sincerely,

Name withheld

....

Dear Name withheld,

This is such a good question, and such a good opportunity to concisely crystallize my thoughts on this issue that I'm going to do it before I finish my first morning cup of tea.

I've learned over the years that there is no better "boomerang" than the energy generated by the karmic reaction to the perpetrator's own unworthy motives and actions. The strength and efficacy of this reaction is proportionally relative to the level of your nonattached "innocence" in the matter.

This is not to say that evoking a goetic demon and using its sigil to zap your enemy might not work. But if done properly, such a working would most likely result in a personal magical adventure in which you'll have to confront (and overcome) terrifying personal issues within yourself; perhaps a life-altering adventure which, in all likelihood, would dwarf any office inconvenience you are trying to avoid in the first place.

If this situation does not merit such a character-building, knock-down, drag-out, battle with your own dark and hidden issues, if you don't believe it is the right moment to provoke a battle to prove to yourself and the cosmos the innocence and integrity of your own motives and actions, then I advise you confront this issue on the same plane it exists right now. It would be far safer and more effective just simply to punch these material-world people in their material-world noses and take the consequences. That would certainly be preferable to disturbing the fragile tranquility of your precious subconscious mind. Are you prepared to take that gamble? Are you in fact *that* undeserving of the slings and arrows of everyday business dealings?

I hope this has been helpful ... and now on to my tea!

Baba Lon

✺

Why Do Some Goetic Magicians Go Mad?

Hello Baba Lon,

We met briefly several years ago during a lecture you gave on Tarot (which included some handouts on goetic affiliations with the Tarot). While you volunteered your time to answer questions after the lecture, and even included an "open-ended" offer to try to respond to questions occurring later, after one had "digested" your material, I found that I had to do quite a bit of research and "steep" for quite a while.

Thus my questions have to do with safety and effectiveness of Goetic evocation.

I note that it has been well documented (by your own comments in your book *Angels, Demons & Gods of the New Millennium* that a lot of "evokers" tend to develop a predilection towards insanity.

In the book you mention in the last chapter your assessment of the phenomenon and your considerations of it. This includes an outline of sorts on how to avoid such pitfalls. I am moved to comment that such a methodology (not "micro-managing" the demon, or [my phrase] "becoming intoxicated; with the Deity energy [authoritative position?]) is apparently a bit challenging for corporate executives, much less a ceremonialist.)

I have noted that most folks who dominate the more colorful exchanges on the internet forums (including the author-magicians "A" and "B") seem to have evoked more than one "critter," and this seems to be a common constituent of their eventual "de-stabilization" both of their physical and mental health.

I also have to wonder aloud if it isn't the strain of attempting physical manifestation that doesn't contribute heavily to these health problems. But I have no real statistical data to corroborate with.

I have to write that I've noticed that your writings only specify an evocation of one: Orobas. And per the references I have, one of his attributes is that he's not only loyal to the exorcist, he protects the same from temptation by other spirits (presumably even other demons).

So I have to ask: Have you managed to evoke more than Orobas? I've read some of the work of Poke Runyon, but only concerning his work with one spirit, Vassago. Have you had or are you aware of any corroboration with other magicians' documentation of the demon plane and their "relative IQ"?

Thank you for your time.

Name withheld

....

Hi Name withheld,

I'm not familiar with (author-magicians "A"'s and "B"'s) work, nor do I participate in or follow online discussions on these matters. I am, however, somewhat familiar with the work, theories, and attitudes of Poke Runyon, and generally find them to be compatible with my "field theory".

While I am not an official member of his organization, I know Poke to be a (if I dare use the term) "sane" individual who has succeeded in carving out a rich and balanced life for himself unencumbered by delusional excesses that often plague those who make magick part of their lives. In other words, Poke has a life ... a life that is enriched by his magical practices but not defined by them. This might be because he was fundamentally wise and balanced* before he even took up the wand and sword; and this might be the key to your concerns. Your questions might have less to do with the number of spirits one calls up and more to do with why one is calling up spirits in the first place.

I know of two individuals who systematically called up all seventy-two goetic spirits over a period of several months. The last time I looked they were both certifiably barking mad. But I don't believe they became mad *because* they evoked all seventy-two spirits ... I believe they were already mad to think they needed to evoke all seventy-two. They were already nuts, and the colorful psycho-drama of Solomonic magick just amplified their existing pathologies by the power of seventy-two.

---

* Poke may take exception to this statement, pointing out his introduction to magick came during a traumatic time in his life as he was dealing with the effects of a serious health issue.

I know for a fact that, over the years, Poke has evoked many more spirits than Vassago. In 1994 I evoked all seventy-two during a formal ceremony that lasted a little over twelve hours (thirty-six in the daylight hours, thirty-six at night) as part of a weekend operation to charge the first deck of my *Tarot of Ceremonial Magick*[*] (that's a story in itself).[†] But once I gave these spirits their charge and embedded them in the cards I did not otherwise retain them in my stable of familiars. That marathon operation not included, I have evoked fewer than a dozen spirits for individual tasks and currently retain only two in an ongoing relationship.

As far as corroboration with other magicians on which spirits are safe or not safe, etc., I'm only mildly interested. I believe that because no two magicians are alike, the spirits ultimately behave differently for each magician. You sound like a thoughtful and competent person. As long as you proceed with confidence and a healthy sense of humor I don't think you have much to fear from this kind of work. But please remember that when you evoke a goetic spirit you are evoking an *adventure*. Living through that adventure turns you into a different person ... the type of person who deserves to receive what you ask from the spirit.

I know this has been too brief, but I hope it has been somewhat helpful.

My best,

Baba Lon

---

* *Ibid.*

† *See* my book, *Low Magick: It's All In Your Head, You Just Have No Idea How Big Your Head Is,* (St Paul, MN: Llewellyn Publications, 2010).

Shouldn't I Be Nice to the Goetic Sprits so They Won't Be Mad at Me and Try to Hurt Me?

Dear Baba Lon,

Hello. I recently read your fascinating and enlightening book, *The Key to Solomon's Key.** Since then it has become recommended reading.

I have some questions about Goetia and magick because I have consciously made the decision to perform an operation once I have gained more information and study.

I don't possess the "tools," so-to-speak, at this point; are there alternatives that you may recommend if one does not have all of the tools necessary for a successful operation?

Also I was wondering what may be the outcome for summoning a spirit without a Triangle, if that spirit was approached respectfully on a conscious level. What I mean is, can the operation be performed in the mind alone with success?

I have read some writers who disagree with your method in the sense that the spirits should not be "commanded" to do things for you. You advocate, at least by my interpretation, "a take charge of the spirits" attitude by the conjurers. Elsewhere I have read (admittedly online at this point) you should approach them in a diplomatic, friendly, accommodating manner. If you approach them in a demanding way they will resist and be more likely to try to will harm on the conjurer.

* Lon Milo DuQuette. *The Key to Solomon's Key: Is This the Lost Symbol of Freemasonry.* (San Francisco, CA: CCC Publishing. Second Edition 2010).

Any info would be greatly appreciated.

Thank you for your time.

Name withheld

....

Dear Name withheld,

I wouldn't worry about fancy tools. I *would*, however, not omit the use of the Circle and a Triangle, at least in magical operations that incorporate the Solomonic formulae. Of course you are certainly free to experiment to your heart's content, especially if *experimentation* is the object of your operation. Simply put, however, if there is no Circle, and no Triangle, there is no Solomonic formula. You'll be doing *another kind* of magick. Doing other kinds of magick is great! Indeed, I believe that true magicians must develop their own techniques based on their own understanding of things.

I guess everyone has their own idea of what goetic spirits are. There are lots of other kinds of spirits that I work with without evoking them into a Triangle. There are lots of other kinds of spirits I don't command. I only use the Triangle with goetic spirits because of my current understanding (accurate or not) of the formulae of this particular magical art form. I only command those spirits who need someone to command them—spirits who are by nature (and tradition) "infernal" in nature. These are blind forces that (when harnessed, controlled and directed) enthusiastically do all of the constructive heavy lifting in the universe, but (when unharnessed, uncontrolled and undirected) destroy things (including bodies, minds, marriages, careers, lives, and self-respect) with the same enthusiastic fierceness and zeal. These are forces I must master in order to master their mirror natures in myself.

Unrecognized, these "spirits" manifest in my life as problems, obstacles, and enemies. I only resort to goetic evocation when I have a problem that needs to be solved; an obstacle needs to be overcome that is hindering my Great Work; a spiritual enemy that needs to be defeated. And in those cases IT IS THE DEMON THAT IS MY PROBLEM. IT IS THE DEMON THAT IS MY OBSTACLE. IT IS THE DEMON THAT IS MY ENEMY! As such, as Levi sings, "... these devils by my might to angels I MUST change. On them must I impose my will ... the law of light."

Once I have a goetic spirit successfully mastered and in my employ I arrange from then on to evoke it without the circle and triangle. As long as it remains loyal I treat it with the utmost respect, courtesy and love. As my initiatory level rises I, in turn, raise its level.

At least that is my Solomonic magick world view and the one I use when I operate goetic evocation. Perhaps your experiments will prompt you to look at things differently. In any case I wish you good luck. I've got to go to bed now.

My best,

Baba Lon

✵

Is it Wise to Evoke Angels or Demons for Financial Help?

Hi Baba Lon,

I have been a fan ever since I first bought your books and Tarot which I came across by chance on Amazon. I must admit I am not much of a magician—my interest has always been in the psychology of change.

I have never seriously attempted the angel and demon stuff since the illustrations in your Illustrated Goetia scared the shit out of me! Some of these guys looked curiously familiar; but then this is a strange neighborhood!

However, my life at 63 is more demanding than ever. My wife died by her own hand five years ago leaving me twin sons to bring up (21 years old). I cared for my wife till her death which meant we lived off savings and I am now broke. I have a new partner and intend picking up my former career as a commercial artist but need money to set the lads up (both were emotionally damaged by their mother's death and have had problems with drugs and the law) in their own place. I also have another son, 31, who is schizophrenic and in and out of the hospital.

My partner and I intend to move south and spend our last years working in our own studio. The only thing that stops us is lack of money.

My question is: would it be wise to ask the angels or demons for help? I have always believed it was wrong to try and use magick for personal gain but unless I get some real money my life is gong to be entirely useless and pointless. It feels like there is something preventing me from achieving my desires. I would appreciate any advice you could toss my way.

Best Wishes

Name withheld

....

Hi Name withheld,

Unless you feel particularly undeserving of success, I see no reason not to apply your magical efforts towards enriching your life and improving your financial/material situation. The fact is, whether your recognize it or not, you are already applying your magical efforts towards those ends. At the moment, however, you're just not doing it very well.

That being said, you may be unknowingly working your magick more successfully in other areas of your life; areas that are perhaps just as (or even more) important than money. It sounds like you've been through some rough times and are still having to deal with some serious challenges. As I'm sure I don't have to tell you, suicide, drugs, cops, and schizophrenia, are in-your-face 'demons' in anyone's book. They are in your life because your dharma or your karma (or whatever you want to call the reasons for your present existence) has put them there. Dealing with these very real demons for one's family (*and one's self*) is as magically heroic as any formal goetic evocation, and certainly renders your life anything but pointless and useless.

If I were to offer any advice based on the few words you've written me, I would counsel that you first make sure the spiritual forces that are already in your life are securely in the "Triangle" and are reasonably under control. Then, determine what you really want. Do you want money? Or do you want the happiness and satisfaction that you think the money will bring to your life? If it is the latter, then work your magick to achieve that. Why evoke a demon for cash if what you *really* need to invoke is a *muse* to charge your golden years with artistic ecstasy?

I'm sure this is not the kind of advice you wanted, but it's the middle of the night and I get preachy. I sincerely wish you the very best of luck.

My best,

Baba Lon

✵

When the Goetic Magician Forgets a Promise

Dear Baba Lon,

First of all let me thank you once more for the great opportunity to visit your classes. They are really very interesting. Your books were always important in my personal library and it's a great opportunity to meet with you in person. I would now like to discuss with you some of a Goetia experience.

I was just starting my Goetia practice three years ago. I made a black mirror, circle, and other stuff, which Poke Runyon described in his book. I spent several months mastering tratakam and autohypnosis.

That time I was evoking Orobas. I decided to ask him to give me new career opportunities. During the evocation I usually can get the spirit's image but often I lose audio-contact. (I'm working on this problem now). I had the same situation that day. Therefore after his coming, which I could see in a mirror, I requested of him to provide me with new career opportunities and promised him to make his sigil on the metal plate "which will last forever" as you described in your Goetia book. I gave him license to depart and closed the temple.

The result of that evocation was very strong. Five to six days later I got a series of phone calls from companies that wanted to hire me on very good conditions. I eventually accepted one of those offers.

What happened after that? I was so busy with the new position that I postponed paying Orobas by making his metal sigil. I delayed payment for at least eight to nine months, which I now see was really stupid from my side.

One day I began to see really strange things happening around me. Initially I had bad dreams that night. During the day when I was walking near electric poles, five to eight crows were literally chasing me, flying from one pole to another and cawing loudly all the time. During the day I noticed some strange conflicts appearing from nowhere. So clearly there was something wrong happening, and after my returning home, I decided to perform the Banishing Ritual of the Pentagram. I just started to do the Qabalistic Cross and when I touched the forth point saying "ve-Gedulah," I was shocked by the loud sound of an explosion just over my head, originating at the point where we usually place Kether during the Middle Pillar exercise. The sound was very loud and dry, as if somebody was sharply tearing old, thick, dry canvas. I was shocked initially, but several minutes later I managed to perform the Ritual of the Pentagram and repeated it several times in every room of my apartment with no sounds that time.

The next weekend I made a metal sigil of Orobas and left it in a forest. The next days after that I began to see signs of strong sympathy from people who initially had strange, unexpected conflicts with me for no reason. Several weeks after that, I made a second sigil of Orobas and again dropped it in a forest.

Although I don't have direct proof that these phenomena were caused by Orobas, I have a strong feeling that it was the work of him or his familiars. It seems I made him upset by delaying payment for so long. What do you think about that? Do you know similar cases of harassment when people were delaying payment to Goetia entities for their done work?

Several months later I was evoking Orobas again. We had reorganization in our company and I asked him for protection and a positive outcome. During that evocation I had a picture, but lost hearing of him. So, I closed the Temple.

The same night I had a dream. A human person who looked like a photo-negative (black face on a white background) came to my dream and calmed me down, giving information about positive outcomes for me after all the chaos of the reorganization. In that case again I had a strong feeling that it was either Orobas or his familiar. It's interesting that he looked like Belial in your Goetia book. So no horse features, but like a person on a photo-negative. What do you think about that?

In your Goetia book you mentioned that results brought by Goetia demons often have a typical demonic, infernal hue. In my case I had it too. Orobas did what I asked him, but the result had such negative aspects, and at some point all that stuff became unacceptable for me.

It's quite interesting how they work. Now I'm working on autohypnosis, and tratakam techniques to improve my hearing abilities, since I sometimes lose audio contact with them while still having visual contact.

Sorry this has been such a long letter, but I would be very interested in your comments about these events. I'm sure you have very extensive Goetia experience.

Thank you very much,

Name withheld

....

Hi Name withheld,

It was nice meeting you last Monday and I hope you can make it to class as often as possible.

Your goetic experiences are very interesting and for the most part characteristic of this kind of operation.

When you charge a spirit to do something for you and promise it something, if it succeeds you are in a sense writing that contract with yourself on the paper of your subconscious mind. Of course that's going to eat at you if you don't uphold your end of the deal, and eventually that attracts unwanted energy and forces around you.

The fact that unpleasant or "infernal" phenomena accompany the fulfillment of your request indicates that your request was initially not well thought out, or it was stated in a way that was not entirely compatible with your own best interests. That's why it's so very important to take great pains to formulate in your own mind what it is you *really* want from the operation.

I am reminded of the time my friend David P. Wilson (S. Jason Black) evoked Paimon for the purpose of securing a particular job with a talent agency in Hollywood. He sacrificed a rat to Paimon and used the blood to sign a most breathtakingly beautiful hand-painted document, a pact, with the spirit. The pact stipulated that if David got the job he would make Paimon an "offering of blood" each month on the anniversary of the evocation.

David got the job, which was a bit more stressful than he imagined. Each day he came home exhausted, his nerves completely shot. Needless to say he forgot to make the monthly sacrifices and at the end of ninety days admitted himself to the hospital emergency room with abdominal pains. The doctor told him he had a "Bleeding Ulcer."

Don't be too concerned if your spirit doesn't neatly match descriptions you've read in books. It has been my experience that a successfully evoked spirit may look much different than how they are described in books or by other magicians. Even the characters and moods of the spirits vary dramatically. My Orobas can be a sweetheart and yours might eat you alive.

It appears that you have a natural talent for this kind of magick, which if used wisely can be an important tool in your quest for enlightenment. I wouldn't, however, think it should be anyone's *only* tool.

Baba Lon

How Much Preparation for an Evocation?

Hi Baba Lon,

I'm a big admirer of your work and have found your latest book to be highly informative; a work which I have often pointed other people to. However, in this book and the excellent *Illustrated Goetia** that you released a while ago, I found no reference to the preparation of the operative. How do you feel about fasting and other acts of purification, such as sexual abstinence, before the work takes place? I ask this, as some grimoires like the Heptameron are adamant that the operative goes on a lengthy fast, etc. What's your view on this?

Name withheld

....

Hello Name withheld,

Thanks for the kind words and for taking the time to write. You ask a very good question and I will try to answer it the best way I can.

I think it is very important to "feel" properly prepared to operate this kind of magick. That could mean different things to different magicians.

On one hand, you're probably not going to feel very magical after a huge meal and a couple of pints. Nor are you likely to possess the necessary wit and physical stamina after an exhausting roll in the hay. We just naturally feel clean,

* Aleister Crowley, Lon Milo DuQuette, Christopher S. Hayat, David P. Wilson. *Aleister Crowley's Illustrated Goetia*. (Scottsdale, AZ: New Falcon Publications, 1992. 2nd rev. ed. 2000, 3rd rev. and expanded ed. 2010).

elevated, and (let's face it) a little more pious with a clean body, empty bowels, and a full sack.

On the other hand, there are times when the circumstances that necessitate the operation conspire to make you at your emotional best to strike out and impose your Will on this situation—when you know in your heart-of-hearts that now is the time to call up this beastie and have it out with him. At times like this you'll know. And it won't matter if your body is filthy, your belly is full, or your ... well, you get the picture.

I guess the key word is "feel." When you have time to prepare, do what it takes to make you "feel" ready to operate. But do not focus so much on the process that you evoke an even more dangerous pair of demons before the operation begins ... I'm talking about the personal demons of vanity and false piety. It's necessary to feel holy when you walk into the circle, but nobody likes a snob, especially the spirits of the Goetia, and believe me, they'll find any chink in your armor.

When you evoke a goetic spirit, you evoke an adventure. Adventures are often scary. But if the hero is true to himself he will be a different person at the end of the adventure. And different things happen to you when you are a different person ... hopefully, one of those things will be the fulfillment of the object of your operation.

Hope this has been helpful,

My best,

Baba Lon

The Holy Guardian Angel

✵

What Is the Straightest Path to the Holy Guardian Angel?

Greetings Baba Lon,

I am very interested in True Will and my Holy Guardian Angel. I know there are paths to it, yet I'm interested in what you think is the straightest path.

Is the philosophy/religion Thelema the best path for someone for whom finding his True Will is all important? I've read *The Book of the Law*. I must be slow. I cannot make heads nor tails of it. Every time I read it, I glean one insight, yet still end up confused.

Thanks,

Name withheld

....

Dear Name withheld,

Good! I'd be really worried if you said you understood *The Book of the Law.* One insight per reading is really a good track record.

> "Let him come through the first ordeal, and it will be
> to him as silver.
> Through the second, gold.
> Through the third, stones of precious water.

Through the fourth, ultimate sparks of the intimate fire."
—Liber AL III:64-67

Knowledge and Conversation of the Holy Guardian Angel is a level of consciousness. The straightest path to the HGA is devotion. If you can fall completely and helplessly in love with God you are there. If this means you find yourself in a loincloth jumping up and down on a street corner blissfully singing Hare Krishna (or Hare Crowley), then so be it. It won't matter to you, because you and the beloved will be joined in ecstatic union.

If, however, you feel in your heart-of-hearts (and that's where the Holy Guardian Angel lives) that you still have *some mission* to accomplish in this incarnation before hopping on the train and taking the "straightest path" to bliss land, then you should start shopping around to see what your mission is and customize your devotional quest for the Angel in order to harmonize and manifest your life's mission (Will).

Thelema is just a path that recognizes the formulae and dynamics of the quest as they generally manifest during this current phase of humanity's consciousness. Thelema provides a certain vocabulary of terms that describe universal concepts that could just as easily be labeled something else. But one does not have to adapt or embrace the Thelemic terms in order to utilize the formulae. Am I making sense?

Thelema is bigger than techniques and religious forms. You don't have to use the techniques and religious forms of Thelema (as you see them practiced today) in order to utilize the Thelemic formulae to discover and do your Will, or gain Knowledge and Conversation of the Holy Guardian Angel or cross the Abyss, or dissolve into Godhead.

Trust your instincts on this matter. Chances are your instincts are the voice of your HGA talking to you right now.

Baba Lon

✹

Do I First Need My HGA Before Beginning any Magick Work?

Dear Baba Lon,

I am a ceremonial magician. I just purchased your Enochian Magick book.

Israel Regardie says in *The Tree of Life* that before you attempt any Goetia you need to be in communion with your HGA. Is the same thing true of Enochian Magick?

Sincerely,

Name withheld

....

Dear Name withheld,

No. From a practical point of view one must start all manner of magical work prior to the full HGA experience. Just keep in mind, however, that all pre-HGA work will be a hit-and-miss affair ... but jeeze! You have to start somewhere!

Baba Lon

✷

Falling in Love with the Holy Guardian Angel

Dear Baba Lon,

I have been increasingly drawn to the idea of "finding" my Holy Guardian Angel. Mentioning this to a friend of mine, he read me the intro to the book on Abramelin the Mage*. Six months as a hermit! Yikes! Then, I thumbed through your book *The Magick of Aleister Crowley* today and found *Liber Samekh*, a ceremony of the Invocation of the HGA as well as a chapter preceding it.

---

* Abraham Von Worms, Georg Dehn, ed., Steven Guth, tran. *The Book of Abramelin: a New Translation*. (Lake Worth, FL: Ibis Press, 2006).

It seems knowledge of one's Holy Guardian Angel would be handy in both life and death, or the passing from one to the other. There are probably other good "uses" for a Holy Guardian Angel. Can you give any practical advice beyond what is in the book, for such a venture in knowing?

And maybe the first question to be answered is: what is an Adept? I have the sense that I may be trying to run before I can stand up.

In appreciation for your knowledge and humor,

Name withheld

....

Dear Name withheld,

Knowledge and Conversation of the Holy Guardian Angel is a love thing. Work on developing the ability to fall hopelessly, blissfully, passionately in love with GOD (or whatever your object of supreme divinity is). Each of us is already trying to mate with our HGA every time we fall in love with someone or something. It's not really the person or object of our devotion we're falling in love with, we're falling in love with a perfected ideal (something that no person or thing could in reality ever live up to). That ideal is the Angel. That perfected ideal is really *us* (a fact we'll discover when we and the Angel are united). Until then, we're already well armed with the only tool we need to lure the Angel to us: intense, insane, romantic naiveté; a devotion so consuming it would embarrass us to death if we weren't so blinded by *Love.*

Hope this has been helpful.

Baba Lon

P.S. If we weren't so impatient to run we would never learn to stand and walk.
P.P.S. My definition of an Adept: a person who is always in over his head ... and loves it! It always seems like you're starting in the middle of things. There *is* no shallow end of the pool. (Gee! I ought to write fortune cookies!)

✵

Is Solitude Necessary to Invoke the Holy Guardian Angel?

Dear Baba Lon,

I have been a fan of your books for some time. I got into western occultism around my late teens due to various bands and rejection of mainstream religion. I found a copy of Crowley's *Book of Thoth* in an old book store along with a pack of tarot cards. I went home and read the book from cover to cover and it did not make a lick of sense. So I kept purchasing other books by him and eventually found out his notorious reputation. I did not mind, because I found your book, *Magick of Aleister Crowley,*[*] a handbook of Crowley's rituals, and I was hooked. I have a few more of your books that I refer to constantly. I eventually ran across the importance of obtaining one's Holy Guardian Angel. I would like to embark upon this task but lack the funds to support myself. So I thought I would ask someone who would know something about this subject.

I do not have anyone who knows anything about occultism other than the mysterious group who hangs in the quad at the University, hustling their accusations of the Illuminati. So I stick with my own research. I eventually came across your

* Lon Milo DuQuette, *The Magick of Aleister Crowley: Handbook of the Rituals of Thelema.* (York Beach, ME: Weiser Books, 2003).

Illustrated Goetia[*] and was amazed that you were bold enough to perform a goetic evocation before you received your HGA. I am also in a position in my life where I lack the funds to grow spiritually and materially. I will get there, but I ask you, is it possible to follow the *Book of Abramelin*[†] and live a life of someone in our day and age? You know, keep my job and keep to my studies while secretly performing the operation, or do you need complete solitude? I'm a man who desperately seeks to perform my will and would accept any form of advice from a man whom I look up to. I would like to thank you for your contribution to Hermetic Magick and putting a little insight into a person like me.

Name withheld

....

Dear Name withheld,

No. I don't think the solitude thing is absolutely necessary unless one is going for the full eighteen-month, by-the-book, pray-till-you-go-crazy-and-get-so-totally-blissed-out-and-drooling-in-love-with-the-HGA-that-the-rest-of-your-life-can-go-to-hell-'cause-it's-all-meaningless-anyway-compared-to-the-love-of-the-HGA operation ... then ... solitude is probably a good idea. Otherwise you've got a life to live, responsibilities to yourself and others that your karma and inherited destiny have presented you. You do the work *however*

* Aleister Crowley, Lon Milo DuQuette, Christopher S. Hyatt, David P. Wilson. *Aleister Crowley's Illustrated Goetia*. 3rd rev. ed. (Scottsdale, AZ: New Falcon Publications, 2010).

† Abraham Von Worms, Georg Dehn, ed., Steven Guth, tran. *The Book of Abramelin: a New Translation*. (Lake Worth, FL: Ibis Press, 2006).

you can, *when* you can, and *if* you can. Keeping focused is the key. When you are truly focused—the work does *you*.

Hope this has been helpful.

Baba Lon

✷

The Holy Guardian Angel in Prison

Dear Baba Lon,

I don't know if you will receive or answer this letter because, as you probably can see by the envelope, I am writing it from within the walls of prison. I am finishing up nearly three years of a drug-related conviction and will soon be transitioning out of here as part of my release cycle.

I have been interested in magick and mysticism since I was a teenager (I am twenty-nine years old) and before my arrest had read Crowley's *Magick in Theory and Practice*[*] (can't say I understood much of *that*!) and his *The Book of Thoth*[†] and *The Qabalah of Aleister Crowley 777* [‡] I also read two books that you and Dr. Hyatt wrote: *The Enochian World of Aleister*

[*] Aleister Crowley, *Magick, Liber ABA: Book Four (part III)*, ed. Hymenaeus Beta, 2nd rev. ed. (York Beach, ME: Weiser Books, 1997).

[†] Aleister Crowley, *The Book of Thoth: A Short Essay on the Tarot of the Egyptians, Being the Equinox Volume III No. V.* (York Beach, ME: Samuel Weiser, Inc. 1974).

[‡] Aleister Crowley, *777 and Other Qabalistic Writings: Including Gematria & Sepher Sephiroth*. ed. Israel Regardie rev. ed. (Boston, MA: Red Wheel Weiser, 1986).

*Crowley** and *The Way of the Secret Lover*†. It is the *Secret Lover* book that I am most interested in because I now see that if I am ever to grow and spiritually evolve in the right way that I must gain knowledge and conversation with my Holy Guardian Angel. I want to perform Liber Samekh and invoke my HGA.

Obviously, I cannot attempt such an operation in my current environment, and I am so very much looking forward to the day and hour when I will be free to begin this great work of self-transformation. I hope to eventually join a Golden Dawn or O.T.O. body, and also become a Freemason like my father, and grandfather, and great grandfather.

I guess I just wanted to first of all thank you and Dr. Hyatt for writing these wonderful books, and then ask you if you had words of advice for someone like me. I really enjoy playing with numbers and words using 777 (I have a paperback of this book here). It is as if the gods are sending me messages. Only trouble is I don't know what good any of these messages are.

[Note: A lengthy and somewhat rambling comment on an array of numerical "coincidences" and "synchronicities" is here omitted.]

Are the gods just playing with me? For the last year I have been working on the name and numbers of an angel who visits me in dreams. Is this my Holy Guardian Angel? If so, it's more like a personal demon who is tormenting me with puzzles. I feel if I can crack his code it will all become clear to me. But there seem to be so many obstacles in my way that it is easy to become discouraged.

---

* Aleister Crowley, Lon Milo DuQuette, Christopher Hyatt, *Enochian World of Aleister Crowley: Enochian Sex Magick.* (Scottsdale, AZ: New Falcon Publications, 1991, 2006).

† Lon Milo DuQuette, Christopher Hyatt, et al, *Sex Magic, Tantra & Tarot: The Way of the Secret Lover.* (Scottsdale, AZ: New Falcon Publications, 1991, 2nd rev. ed. 2008).

If you don't write back I'll understand, but I thought I'd at least give it a try.

Name withheld

....

Hi Name withheld,

Good to hear you will be transitioning out of that place soon and that your focus is on self-transformation.

You may be surprised when I tell you that even when the magician is out and "free"... even when the magician is able to be part of the work of magical or Masonic groups ... even when the magician is able to have fellowship with others of similar interests and aspirations ... the magician always remains solitary as far as his or her Great Work is concerned.

You will never be more "free" to do the real work than you are right now. You will never be closer to discovering who you are and what it's all about than you are right now ... illumination will never be closer to you than it is right now. So try to see what it is you need to do for yourself right now and do it. It is probably something that seems at first to have nothing to do with magick or Qabalah or gods or angels.

Start with the little things. They are the biggest obstacles. If you smoke or abuse your body in other ways ... stop. You'd like to be able to achieve some level of illumination while you still have four parts to your soul. If you've lost your sense of humor ... get it back. Start to see the universal joke in things ... that's how the heaviest "AHAs!" will be delivered.

You seem fixated at the moment with the spelling of the name and the numeric equivalent of this angelic visitor. Have you thought that the big "message" here was not that you had to somehow crack a code of some qabalistic puzzle to get an answer ... but that the "message" was clearly delivered to you

...THE PUZZLE IS THE ANSWER. Shit yes! Your HGA is a "huge personal demon" of yours! That's why it's the key to your getting your personal, magical, spiritual, and incarnational shit together.

Try harder by not trying so hard. Use the Ruach's qabalistic number games to hone your Neschamah, not drive it! Once you've received your intuitional message move on ... move forward. For Christ's sake! Don't keep picking a word or number to death with gematria, 'cause it's your own life and sanity you'll be picking to death (not to mention the friends you'll bore to death with your ramblings!).

The HGA desires union with you infinitely more than you think you want union with *it*. If you truly realized that, then you would not need *Liber Samekh* or books or orders or gematria, you would just have to swoon and fall into *its* arms. It is standing right behind you, right now, and always screaming at you to just wake up a little and back gently into *it*. You're over-thinking the process ... over-working the process. It's the Anahata chakra, for Christ's sake! You need to fall hopelessly in love with the god-damned Angel. Have you forgotten how to fall in love? Is that one of the little things you need to work on? If so, I suggest you start right now. You two will make a beautiful couple—and you both will still have a lot of work to do as a team.

Hope this has been helpful.

Baba Lon

Is the Holy Guardian Angel Just Me?

Dear Baba Lon,

It has been a long time, but many years ago you and your lovely wife gave me a fantastic dinner after my O.T.O. Minerval Degree and then again at my First Degree about a year later. Sorry I've been out of touch.

I decided after twelve years I wasn't getting any younger and that the most important thing I could do, should do, this incarnation, was slug away at finding my Holy Guardian Angel. Yet Israel Regardie says in his book, *Ceremonial Magic,** almost no one finds this angel. And what if this Holy Guardian Angel is only me—the "Me of Me's"—and I am just the incarnating personality?

Your brother,
Name withheld

....

Dear Name withheld,

"And what if this Holy Guardian Angel is only me—the "Me of Me's"—and I am just the incarnating personality?"

My friend, in my martini-damaged brain's opinion, your statement/question is profoundly on the money. We've chosen this body, this mind, this personality, these warts, and these flaws to be the outward expression of the "Me of Me." It's a game of hide-and-seek we play with ourselves. Me will win when Me gets caught. Then, like loving children or playful

* Israel Regardie, *Ceremonial Magic: A Guide to the Mechanisms of Ritual.* (London: Aeon Books. 2nd ed 2006).

lovers, Me and Me will hug tight and whirl in ecstatic giggles. All of the magick, meditations, and rituals are just clumsy exercises to get us to a place where we realize that, more than anything else in life, we want to *get caught*.

Love,

Baba Lon

✳

Have You Performed the Abramelin Operation?

Dear Baba Lon,

I have been meaning to ask you if you have ever performed the Abramelin operation. I know you speak of the Holy Guardian Angel in your class and you sound like you have more knowledge and conversation than most. Is the Abramelin how you achieved it?

Also, what is your opinion on the age restriction in the Abramelin operation? As of now it looks like I won't be able to attempt it until I'm older than is permitted due to family, children, etc. I'm thinking that the requirement is mainly because back when the book was written, people that age were considered ancient and were often infirmed and could not physically carry on for the prescribed time. That is no longer the case. Thoughts?

Name withheld

....

Dear Name withheld,

No. I haven't done the Abramelin operation per se. As far as Knowledge and Conversation of my Holy Guardian Angel goes, I've certainly not experienced anything like what is described in the Abramelin text. If I am a $5^\circ = 6^\square$ on the Tree of Life, I've achieved it some other way and it is manifesting in my life in such a way as to be unrecognizable in Abramelin terms.

Don't look at the book of Abramelin as a recipe book. The procedure as described lays out a basic formula for a successful operation. It is not unlike other techniques used by devotional aspirants of all cultures and religions. Don't worry so much about the details but try to grasp the general formula. Arrange your life in such a way as to make yourself worthy to become who you really are.

Baba Lon

Real Life

✷

Balancing Family Life and Magick

Good Evening Baba Lon,

I'm hoping for some guidance from a master. How did you balance magical study and raising a family? From everything I've seen, you seem to have the whole darn thing figured out.

I do not even have a family yet, and I struggle with maintaining a balance between my esoteric studies, my work, and regular living. I can't even imagine adding in parent/teacher meetings, soccer, etc. let alone introducing the idea of Thelema to children while surrounded by conservatives.

I would love to know what your secret is here. I love my esoteric work, and I love my job. I don't mind being alone to work, but it must be unhealthy to the degree I've found myself in.

I'm sure I'm not the only one looking to find out how to balance this, and you seem to have done it as masterfully as anything else.

Any advice would be sincerely appreciated.

Yours respectfully,
Name withheld

....

Dear Name withheld,

You ask an excellent question, but I'm afraid you have begun with a defective observation. I don't *have the whole thing*

figured out. I did not have it figured out in my youth; I do not presently have the whole thing figured out; nor is it likely I will ever have the whole thing figured out. As a matter of fact, the older I get the less about life I seem to understand and the less important understanding it all seems be. (I must also add that the older I get the more I simply appreciate the entire experience for whatever it *is*!)

My attitude might be the result of creeping senility or it might be the onset of that degree of illumination I once-upon-a-time convinced myself was the only goal in life worth striving for. (Perhaps senility and illumination are one and the same thing.)

Please forgive me, but to address your question I'm going to cut and paste a little clip from something I wrote in the opening of one of my books,* and for a little speech I delivered to an O.T.O. National Conference.† I hope it will be helpful.

> I'm not a *WISE* man. I'm a *LUCKY* man. To my *Tree of Life* should be added a fourth Pillar ... the *Pillar of Luck*; To the mystic formulas of I N R I and LVX and NOX I must add FELIX, the Latin word meaning "Lucky" ... because, even though my life might appear to be characterized by a series of *wise* actions and decisions, it is in reality merely peppered by freakish moments of unbelievable *good luck*.
>
> In the East they would call my lifestyle that of the "householder." I'm married and have for my entire adult life endeavored (with varying degrees of success) to provide a loving and stable environment for my family. Things have worked out pretty well, but not because I am wise. In truth, throughout the years I've been lucky to have a sainted wife and beloved son who have provided *me* with a loving and stable environment.
>
> I wasn't acting *wisely* forty-two years ago when I took far too much LSD out in Joshua Tree National Monument, and vowed to the multiple red rising suns that I would not return from the desert until I was a holy man.
>
> Later that same day, it wasn't *wisdom* that oozed like melting psychedelic wax down the wallpaper

* Lon Milo DuQuette, *Enochian Vision Magick: An Introduction and Practical Guide to the Magick of Dr. John Dee and Edward Kelley* (San Francisco: Red Wheel/Weiser, 2008), xxxviii.

† Lon Milo DuQuette, *To Beauty and Strength We Must Add Wisdom*. From Beauty and Strength: Proceedings of the Sixth Biennial National Ordo Templi Orientis Conference, Salem, Massachusetts, August 10-12, 2007 E.V. (Riverside, CA: Ordo Templi Orientis, Supreme Grand Council, 2009), 34.

of that little beer bar in Costa Mesa as I pondered the nature of space-time and suddenly realized the inescapable "rightness" of spending the rest of my life with Constance Olson, my high school sweetheart.

And it wasn't *wisdom* that sent me careening past the pool table to the payphone by the pinball machine, and call her in Nebraska to ask her to marry me. (I think, however, it *was* wise that I waited until our twentieth wedding anniversary to confess I proposed to her while frying my brains out on acid.)

Fate (coupled with a conspicuous lack of ambition) has conspired to make our lifestyle one of genteel poverty (well, not always so genteel). We've never owned a house, a new car, or a credit card. On the other hand, we've always lived in moderately affluent communities and safe neighborhoods. We've always owned old cars that usually get us where we're going. Our bills consist exclusively of the rent, the utilities, and health insurance. Our only expenses are groceries and gasoline.

Our only debts are those we can never repay—debts to dear friends and brethren for treasures of love and support. Such kindness has allowed us to travel the world and do many things we could not otherwise afford.

Some people say that's a miracle. I agree. Miracles are part of my job. I am a magician … and I'm *lucky.*

So there it is. I know that's probably not the kind of response you wanted to hear. But it's the over-riding answer to your question. I'm the laziest man in the world. I'm so lazy that I cannot abide expending one ounce of energy or performing one iota of labor that is not in some way an expression of my passion for enlightened happiness. Perhaps looking at it from the outside it might seem like a *tour de force* that masterfully balances family and esoteric study, career and magical practice, but what's really going on is that I'm being almost pathologically selfish and lazy! In fact, until you brought it up it never occurred to me that there was any balancing act going on at all.

The school plays, the PTA meetings, the lousy jobs, the bills, the illnesses, the landlords were every bit as much a part of my magical life as the evocations, invocations and initiations … in fact they *were* initiations!

Joseph Campbell said it all when he said, "Follow your bliss." Follow your bliss, and the balancing act will take care of itself.

That's about as wise as I can wax ten minutes before going to bed. If this hasn't been helpful, I hope it at least made you smile.

Baba Lon

✷

Addiction/Forgiveness

Dear Baba Lon,

I really enjoyed reading your autobiography. You have led, and are leading, a very extraordinary life. Within that life you have overcome many obstacles. I have an obstacle in my way that has hounded me for nearly my entire life. I am a sex addict. I know that you have no problems with sex, on any moral ground. This isn't about morality; it's about me being controlled by something that doesn't make me happy. Depression, drugs, and alcohol have been a constant in my life for nearly eighteen years now. It would be great if you could maybe point me towards some help. What are your views on addiction?

Thank you for your time,

Name withheld

....

Dear Name withheld,

I'm glad you enjoyed *My Life with the Spirits** and have taken the time to write me.

Let me begin by saying that I am profoundly unqualified to offer any advice to anyone on issues of health or psychology. If I were to offer any suggestion it would be what I'm sure you've heard a thousand times before: that is, to seek the counsel of a licensed professional.

I too struggle everyday with a variety of issues that I handle with uneven levels of success. If I've accomplished anything it has been the partial ability to accept myself *as I am*—from day to day, second to second.

Recently I found myself riding in a car with three other authors (professional writers who are far more celebrated and successful than myself I assure you) who were sharing their feelings of guilt concerning their "bad" behavior and what they considered their weaknesses, character flaws, addictions, etc. As I listened I thought to myself how *my* weaknesses, character flaws, addictions, etc. were far more serious than theirs but I wasn't struggling with *any* of the guilt. For a moment I was starting to feel guilty that I wasn't *feeling* guilty; but then I realized why there was no guilt. When there was a

* Lon Milo DuQuette, *My Life with the Spirits* (York Beach, ME: Weiser Books, 1999).

break in their chatter I told them in a goofy dramatic voice, "I've learned to forgive myself."

Everyone laughed very hard for a moment, and then the car went silent.

It's true. I've learned to forgive myself. But by doing so I've also installed within myself a governor on my behavior—a governor who is (always at least trying) to make sure that I remain worthy of that forgiveness. I don't think I could tolerate it if that governor were some other person or organization or religion or philosophy. My instant reaction to that would be one big "Fuck You!" Saying "Fuck You" to myself, on the other hand, is a different matter and definitely sets me to thinking.

Now this doesn't mean that I don't misbehave anymore. On the contrary, I still habitually .... *(something embarrassingly naughty)*; and I haven't completely stopped .... (*something even more embarrassingly naughty*); every once in awhile I even .... *(something I would never discuss with strangers)*! But I no longer indulge in these things "unduly." I no longer fall thoughtless into my actions, even when body chemistry is involved. This has resulted in a marked decline in such behavior, and that's good for my health, stability and general well-being. However, that's only a byproduct of the real payoff. The real reward comes from the fact that the concept of "control" has ceased to be an issue altogether. Now I can reserve guilt for important things, like being a year behind deadline for a book I've already been paid for!

I hope this has been helpful and I wish you the very best luck with your life.

My best,

Baba Lon

Lose Your Soul?

Hello Baba Lon,

I've been interested in Magick for some time now and I think I'm ready to "dive in." However, I'm still having a few nagging questions that are difficult to find the answers to in books on the subject.

Knowing that your expertise is in Enochian (Angel) Magick, in your opinion, how does this differ from being a born again (true) Christian? Also, on the other side of the coin, are you familiar enough with the working of the "dark side" of Majick (sic) to know whether a person could lose his soul or become "demon possessed" by dabbling in that particular discipline?

I've read many things about it—both good and bad.

Thank you.

Name withheld

....

Hi Name withheld,

Forgive the brevity of my answer this morning. I've got a lot on my plate today. I'm going to be perfectly frank with you, and I want you to take what I'm about to say in the spirit that it is offered.

They say there is no such thing as a bad question, and your questions certainly aren't exceptions. But they do indicate to me that your fundamental understanding of the subject is currently such that you are probably mistaken in your assertion that you are "... ready to dive in" to magick.

I don't know how to answer your first question. Dee was a Christian, as were many Medieval and Renaissance magicians. Whether they were "True Christians" is something upon which I don't feel qualified to pass judgment. Perhaps if you read my books, *The Key to Solomon's Key,*[*] or *Enochian Vision Magick,*[†] you might get a clearer idea. Also, for the fundamentals, my *Angels, Demons & Gods of the New Millennium*[‡] might be helpful.

People with existing emotional or mental issues should stay away from guns, drugs, alcohol, magick, and Christianity. If you're crazy to begin with all these things make it worse.

I've never experienced a case of "demon" possession outside a tavern or cocktail lounge, and in those instances the possessed individuals had never in their lives dabbled in magick at all.

I do not wish to offend you, but if you are disturbed by the possibility (or even the "capability") of *losing your soul* or being *demon possessed*, then it is likely you are currently not in touch with the spiritual realities that would make magick a safe and meaningful endeavor.

My best,

Baba Lon

---

* Lon Milo DuQuette, *Key to Solomon's Key: Is This The Lost Symbol of Freemasonry* (San Francisco: CCC Publishing, Second revised edition, 2010).

† Lon Milo DuQuette, *Enochian Vision Magick* (York Beach, ME: Weiser Books, 2008).

‡ Lon Milo DuQuette, *Angels, Demons & Gods of the New Millennium* (York Beach, ME: Weiser Books, 1997).

✺

Is Magick Harmful to Children?

Dear Baba Lon,

My wife asked me a question about the *Necronomicon*[*] the other day, as she has been doing angel magick through talismans and has had little success, so she intends to use the *Necronomicon*. She asked me if it would be dangerous with a small child in the house if it even works. I don't know if it's a good idea or not, as I have never used that mythos; I have read the book, but I don't know if it works. Could you offer some opinions or advice about that system? Have you ever used it, does it work and is there any danger to it (especially to our daughter)? I remember from your book you used the Goetia when your child was young. Would you have used the *Necronomicon* instead?

Name withheld

---

* From Wikipedia: "The ***Necronomicon*** is a fictional grimoire appearing in the stories by horror writer H.P. Lovecraft and his followers. It was first mentioned in Lovecraft's 1924 short story "The Hound," written in 1922, though its purported author, the "Mad Arab" Abdul Alhazred, had been quoted a year earlier in Lovecraft's "The Nameless City." Among other things, the work contains an account of the Old Ones, their history, and the means for summoning them" The Wikipedia article also goes on to mention "modern editions"; "The line between fact and fiction was further blurred in the late 1970s when a book purporting to be a translation of the "real Necronomicon" was published. This book, by the pseudonymic "Simon," had little connection to the fictional Lovecraft Mythos but instead was based on Sumerian mythology. It was later dubbed the "Simon Necronomicon". Going into trade paperback in 1980 it has never been out of print and has sold 800,000 copies by 2006 ...". In 2008, my friends at Ibis Press issued their beautiful 31st Anniversary edition of Simon's book, with a limited leatherbound numbered edition available as well.

Liber Resh vel Helios sub figura CC

0. These are the adorations to be performed by aspirants to the A∴A∴.

1. Let him greet the Sun at dawn, facing East, giving the sign of his grade. And let him say in a loud voice: Hail unto Thee who art Ra in Thy rising, even unto Thee who art Ra in Thy strength, who travellest over the Heavens in Thy bark at the Uprising of the Sun. Tahuti standeth in His splendour at the prow, and Ra-Hoor abideth at the helm. Hail unto Thee from the Abodes of Night!

2. Also at Noon, let him greet the Sun, facing South, giving the sign of his grade. And let him say in a loud voice: Hail unto Thee who art Ahathoor in Thy triumphing, even unto Thee who art Ahathoor in Thy beauty, who travellest over the heavens in thy bark at the Mid-course of the Sun. Tahuti standeth in His splendour at the prow, and Ra-Hoor abideth at the helm. Hail unto Thee from the Abodes of Morning!

3.Also, at Sunset, let him greet the Sun, facing West, giving the sign of his grade. And let him say in a loud voice: Hail unto Thee who art Tum in Thy setting, even unto Thee who art Tum in Thy joy, who travellest over the Heavens in Thy bark at the Down-going of the Sun. Tahuti standeth in His splendour at the prow, and Ra-Hoor abideth at the helm. Hail unto Thee from the Abodes of Day!

4.Lastly, at Midnight, let him greet the Sun, facing North, giving the sign of his grade, and let him say in a loud voice: Hail unto thee who art Khephra in Thy hiding, even unto Thee who art Khephra in Thy silence, who travellest over the heavens in Thy bark at the Midnight Hour of the Sun. Tahuti standeth in His splendour at the prow, and Ra-Hoor abideth at the helm. Hail unto Thee from the Abodes of Evening.

5. And after each of these invocations thou shalt give the sign of silence, and afterward thou shalt perform the adoration that is taught thee by thy Superior. And then do thou compose Thyself to holy meditation.

6. Also it is better if in these adorations thou assume the God-form of Whom thou adorest, as if thou didst unite with Him in the adoration of That which is beyond Him.

7. Thus shalt thou ever be mindful of the Great Work which thou hast undertaken to perform, and thus shalt thou be strengthened to pursue it unto the attainment of the Stone of the Wise, the Summum Bonum, True Wisdom and Perfect Happiness.

"Will" is a brief dialogue said before meals.

Leader: *(knocks 3-5-3)* Do what thou wilt shall be the whole of the Law.
All: What is thy will?
Leader: It is my will to eat and to drink.
All: To what end?
Leader: That I may fortify my body thereby.
All: To what end?
Leader: That I may accomplish the Great Work.
All: Love is the law, love under will.
Leader: *(knocks once)* Fall to!

....

Dear Name withheld,

I'm really not trying to take the color and romance out of magick for you, but you should know that the so-called *Necronomicon* that is being sold today in various editions was artfully created in the late 1970s by several people known to myself. In fact, my son has a signed first edition from one of the participants in the project who is a family friend.

That being said, the *Necronomicon*, when used properly, can probably be as viable a system of magical evocation as any number of "ancient" grimoires. Does that surprise you? After all, even the books of the classic *Key of Solomon* had to be created by somebody.

Magick isn't harmful to children, but parents who behave overly dramatic, spooky, fearful and superstitious often are.

I did lots of magical rituals and ceremonies in the house when our son was growing up. I even evoked spirits in his bedroom (with him out of the room, naturally). I did *not*, however, perform serious magick in front of him (with the exception of saying "Will"[*] before eating, 'Resh' at sunrise, noon, sunset, and midnight[†] and going to Gnostic Mass). Neither did Constance and I attempt to turn him into a little magician. I think it's absolutely shameful to see parents who themselves do not yet have an adequate understanding of magick or the nature of their own spiritual explorations trying to indoctrinate their kids.

When Jean-Paul was growing up, Constance and I just tried to be as normal as we could. Kids like normal. But that doesn't mean that normal can't be fun, colorful and interesting. We didn't make a big thing about how "different" we were because we didn't believe in Jesus like the neighbors do. In fact, we exposed him to as many religions and spiritual philosophies as his age would handle. Kids are smart. They can see through Christianity, but they can also see through you and me! Best to teach by the example of your own happiness. If your magick is not making you happy, your kids are certainly not going to want to embrace it when they've grown.

Off my soap box ... got to get ready for Monday night Magick class.

My best,

Baba Lon

✷

Suicide

Hello Baba Lon,

Sorry to bother you on this humid Monday morning, but I was wondering if you have time for a quick (I think) question.

---

* See page 147.

† See page 146.

I was wondering when you die, where are you suppose to go if you do the Thelema thing, or do you just stop existing, or is there another life or something?

Also, are there rules like if you're Christian and you commit suicide you can't get into heaven? If I don't make sense, or you don't wanna bother, that's cool, but I'm trying to figure some stuff out with little success.

Have a great day ... thank you for being nice to me and putting up with all my stupidity.

Name withheld

....

Dear Name withheld,

The honest answer is, I don't know, and neither does anyone else.

The Book of the Law says, "Aye! feast! rejoice! there is no dread hereafter."*

Does that mean there is no *dread* hereafter? Or there is no dread *hereafter*? Or both? Or something altogether different?

One thing we as Thelemites *do* deal with is the concept of the "consciousness of the continuity of existence." The question of whether or not we retain the consciousness of the continuity of our existence, or if it is something that needs to be developed over time and incarnations, I don't know. The Egyptians and the Tibetans seem to suggest it is something to shoot for.

I don't believe in the classic Christian concept of heaven and hell. I do, however, know that we don't understand the nature of consciousness, and that in altered states of consciousness, such as the death coma, time does not behave

* *Liber AL vel Legis (The Book of the Law),* Chapter II, verse 44.

the way it does when we are fully *alive* and not in the death coma. I believe that pleasant or unpleasant experiences can occur to us depending upon the state of mind of the expiring individual.

I believe we all have the right to die when and how we will, and that suicide is not in every case the wrong exit method. However, I believe if a person commits suicide while his or her mind is unbalanced or tormented or fearful, that increases the chances of unpleasantness during the death coma and would likely interfere with the natural flow of things.

In other words, I believe if one is resolved to end one's life, one should be joyful and at peace with the idea that this is absolutely the best moment to begin a new and wonderful adventure. However, if we are doing it because we are bummed out we are probably just going to make things worse.

Hope this has been helpful.

My best,
Baba Lon

✷

Why Am I Doing This Stuff?

Dear Baba Lon,

I'm hoping you may be able to point me in the right direction.

I am trying, without proper direction, to turn my nearly worthless ass into a half-decent magician. I'd even settle for "kind of a magician." At forty years old, I need to do something.

Right now, I've structured my own program ... I think, anyway, by reading and attempting to work through a variety of books, including a nice collection of your work. The thing is, I have no idea what I'm doing. I'm starting to develop some sense of order out of the madness, but I know I'm going to need some guidance. I'm not even sure what to expect from a ritual like the Lesser Banishing Ritual of the Pentagram, although a sense of peace and stillness certainly arrives.

That brings me to the purpose of writing you. I really don't know anyone else anywhere that would know the answer to this, but is there some sort of good mystery school right around the.......... area? Am I being premature in thinking about affiliating? Is it even really necessary?

Thanks for your time. If I don't hear from you, that's cool. I know you must be extremely busy.

Name withheld

....

Hi Name withheld,

I certainly sympathize with your predicament, and unfortunately I don't have much information for you.

There is a fine O.T.O. Lodge in .... That may be the closest O.T.O. body.

Even if you were to affiliate with a magical group, however, you would still be doing the essential work by yourself. If it is any comfort to you, please know that no magician on earth (if they are sane and truthful with themselves) will confess to being anything other than "kind of a magician."

It's good that you've structured your own program, and believe me, it may be years (perhaps never) before it dawns on you *why* you are doing all this stuff.

The basic rituals are designed as metaphors of your evolving/expanding consciousness. Getting comfortable with the Pentagram rituals is getting you comfortable in the world as it appears—a flat earth with a sun that comes up and goes down. The Pentagram helps you master the elements of that world. It's basic. It's a simplistic and inaccurate view of the universe and your place in it. But you've got to start somewhere. Moving to the Hexagram rituals should expand your consciousness from the earth to the sun. Other rituals expand you beyond that, etc.

Whenever you think you are not going anywhere with this stuff ask yourself if you would trade places with the "you" of ten years ago, or five years ago, or last month. You are too close to yourself to know what you know (that's why teachers teach—to find out what they know). You're too close to yourself to be aware of your own changes in consciousness.

Is there a local bar you used to frequent in your twenties but haven't visited in years? Pay it a visit (if you dare) and tell me you don't feel like Christian-fucking-Rosenkreutz compared to the poor souls trapped in the smoky amber of that land-locked ship of fools.

That's about all I have time to confuse you with this morning. I've got a pretty full day ahead of me trying to figure out what I know and wondering why I'm not doing more with the information to make my life and the world a better place.

My best,

Baba Lon

Miscellaneous Technical Matters

✵

Abramelin and Holy Awe

Hello Baba Lon,

Well, I finally found my way (I'm sure you'll hear my two somewhat desperate voicemail messages at some point tonight, about being lost) and wanted to thank you for receiving me into your home.

I've just begun reading your book *Enochian Vision Magick*. I am somewhat new to ceremonial magic (certainly in a practical sense), though I have read (over the span of several decades) a variety of different materials ... philosophical, pagan and otherwise (including *Magick Without Tears*[*] and some of other Crowley's work, though quite a while ago, and it mostly made my head hurt much the same way Kafka's Metamorphosis did the first time I read it). I also am in possession of the *Thoth Tarot* deck as well as the book, though I have not used them for quite some time. I've discovered an affinity for runes and have been using those, mostly, as of late, and I never have become particularly proficient at correlating cards in a spread, though it is something that I aspire to.

I've ordered the book and should receive it in a couple of days. Since I don't really know you, and this is my first glimpse of your take on this type of material, I was trying to assess your view on the material covered tonight. One of the reasons that

* Aleister Crowley, *Magick Without Tears* (Scottsdale, AZ: New Falcon Publications, 1991).

I've shied away from ceremonial (anything) is that it involves a whole lot of memorization. Thus, it might not come as a huge surprise that mathematics was not a strong suit (much to my parents' chagrin, who were both exceptionally good at it). And actions done by rote without understanding and resonance somehow echo of emptiness to my mind, which pretty much cuts a swath through most organized religions.

I suppose that my fascination with esoterica (and currently the vagaries of Ceremonial Magick, Enochian or otherwise) is really to understand myself, or rather the world (universe?) and my place in it ... and perhaps discover that I have, in some minute way, a purpose ... a bit part in a greater whole.

During the course of the reading tonight you mentioned something about touching the reverence/awe within, seeing that many of us in modern day times do not have the reverence for godhead that our forebears did. So ... my question would be ... is it possible to practice this form of magick without utilizing the recommended "worshipful countenance"? I can easily find a "loving/compassionate countenance" but less a worshipful one ... if that makes sense. I hear: the disdain that the originators of the text (Abramelin the Mage, Abraham the Jew, and whoever wrote the Keys of Solomon) hold towards most everyone who is not a "true" follower of Adonai ... discounting all other practices as being invalid ... parlor tricks, almost.

So, with what appears to be great familiarity with the purported creator of humanity, how is it that you know Belial to be a pain in the ass (just wondering)? :) I have only rather recently grasped the role of the "fallen angels" in mankind's progression, and so question the content of the materials that we are reading in correlation to that. I also am quite fascinated in their offspring being genetically linked to the surviving human gene pool, and what effects that might have on us as a race.

I've struggled with many Biblical concepts over time (read about as long ago, or perhaps even further back, as the Crowley material), and reconciling the contradicting materials within the scriptures on the nature of God and every other thing therein. I'd love nothing more than to pull up a chair and pour us both a nice cuppa tea and chat Him up. I feel like I'm trying to fit the pieces of a billion piece puzzle together, and can't find the box cover to look at for reference. I (rather undisciplinedly) meditate ... I occasionally manage to hold my concentration in a disciplined enough manner so as to commune with my guides (which part of me thinks myself daft even acknowledging them real past the confines of my mind, whatever mind is), but quite frequently feel rather overwhelmed with the massive amount of esoteric information available for consumption, some of it contradictory in nature, and some of it rather dubious at best. I often have "I can't believe I ate the whole thing" moments ... and of course feel like falling back into a state of semi-comatose sleep is preferable to trying to digest it all. So I guess I've been on a mission to find the proverbial bottle of spiritual Pepto-Bismol.

Well ... now that I've carried on and most of this must sound like so much gibberish, I will stop here and hope that some of my thoughts made sense, and that you might have some insightful comments.

Thanks again ... and best regards,

Name withheld

....

Dear Name withheld,

Glad you finally made it to Monday night Magick class.

These are wonderful questions and observations and exactly the kind of issues that I wanted this class series to bring to the surface. And hopefully by the time we're through many of these things will be a little clearer.

You ask, "... is it possible to practice this form of magick without utilizing the recommended "worshipful countenance"?

Maybe I over (or under) stated the concept.

I can imagine when the great naturalist, John Muir, first hiked into Yosemite and saw the soft orange light of the rising sun hit the summit of one of those magnificent peaks, he just about crapped his jeans with stunned, wordless awe. It was a transcendent moment ... an epiphany ... an expansion of consciousness in which he somehow realized a greater reality and his place in it.

Or imagine you are awakened in the middle of the night by a strange light coming from your living room and you quietly creep out to discover Buddha sitting serenely on the carpet, and in the glow of His presence you are enveloped by the same infinite joy, sorrow, compassion, love, bliss, and understanding His illumination represents....

Are these experiences (or a thousand other scenarios of "worshipful countenance" you could dream up) beyond your ability to imagine? My guess is your answer is "no." And to make magick of this nature work one needs to develop the power of imagination *that* intense, and the ability to "put" oneself in *that* frame of mind (if that's what we need to call it) at precisely the right moment.

Using the metaphors of magick, if you can't be in awe of the great *whatever it is* then the spirits (the forces that do all the heavy lifting in the universe) will be unable to be in awe of *you*.

In the book Abraham the Jew achieves this attitude with what I consider to be a naive superstitious spiritual world view. In a way he is lucky not to have modern science and cosmology (and, in places, *common sense)* complicate his access to his devotional weapons (one does not have to understand how a gun works in order to pick it up and shoot it).

We, on the other hand must poke around for more rational ways to get ourselves there.

Please forgive all the parentheticals. It's early, and my flow of consciousness is popping my words out parenthetically.

Hope to see you next Monday.

My best,

Baba Lon

The Wand or the Sword?

Dear Baba Lon,

I've been finding your books are indeed treasure-troves of information, and not simply "beginner books," as many seem to think. I was hoping you could clarify one quick point, however.

You state, I believe in your illustrated Goetia (forgive me if I am wrong, as I've been reading four of your books at once, or close together), that the magician should use a wand rather than a sword. I am a bit perplexed by this, as it seems the sword is traditional, and it seems even with the O.T.O., is the tool of choice.

Could you please elaborate on why you suggest the wand over the sword? You state that the sword is useful for intimidation, but I really believed there was more to it than that ... Also, it would seem if the sword was indeed useful for intimidation, than using your methods, the sword would be the preference. I come to this conclusion based on the seemingly hostile manner in which you deal with Goetic demons (*i.e.* threats, a "my way or I'll kill you" mentality, and lack of equal consideration, except upon your own terms).

I hope you can clarify this, as even after additional study, I am still quite perplexed. I am about to embark upon my very first goetic working using a structured format, so I am definitely interested in making it as effective as possible. Would really appreciate any insight you can provide. And I also wanted to personally thank you for your hard work and effort, and let you know that next to Crowley, I consider your work to be the most important to be familiar with as a Thelemite, or even an occultist in general.

Name withheld

....

Hi Name withheld,

Please don't be too perplexed. In fact, don't be perplexed at all. When perplexed, use your instincts, and in this case your instincts are very good.

I conjure with the wand. It is my will, it is the weapon of my Chiah (the part of my soul that is my ultimate self, identical, or at least the miniature version of the supreme consciousness), it's the highest weapon I pull off the shelf representing the highest me I am, and that's what I want to show the beasties first. But you are right. Solomonic magick is a formula of intimidation, and whenever I need to re-conjure a disobedient spirit I do indeed use the sword. (I'll even use the sword to dangle the burning box over the flame in the triangle when things get ugly.)

That's just how I'm comfortable doing things. It's like ..."Look here, mister demon, it is my true divine Self (wand) who conjures you into the Triangle; not my mind (sword) which 90 percent of the time wanders all over the place; not my heart (cup) that 90 percent of the time blinds my common sense; not my body (disk) that fucks with me most of the time ... but the real me!"

If you feel comfortable using the sword to represent the real you for the initial conjuration, please do so with impunity and full confidence. For you it is the equivalent of me using the wand.

Please always keep in mind that your magick is *your magick* and that the rationale for how things should be done ultimately is yours. If your operation succeeds it will be because it was truly your will that it succeeds. If it blows up in your face it will be because of a temporary flaw in your will and not because you used your weapons differently than Baba Lon does.

Good luck and give 'em hell!

Baba Lon

✷

I'M BEING MAGICALLY ATTACKED!

Dear Baba Lon,

Since I started to read books about magick and the occult I feel like I am being psychically/magically attacked. My friend tells me I should protect myself from the evil spirits who want to prevent me from working with God's good angels to help the world and mankind. What spells or rituals can I do to protect myself against evil spirits and black magicians who are trying to destroy me?

Name withheld.

....

Dear Name withheld,

I believe you as yet do not have a mature and realistic understanding of what magick is and what it is not. While I don't believe that there is no such thing as psychic attack, I think in this case you have simply fallen victim to your own superstition and fear.

Personally, I've discovered that the best protection against magical attack is to do absolutely nothing and seek infinite refuge in one's own innocence.

Baba Lon

✵

Do Banishing Rituals Really Work?

Hey Baba Lon,

After practicing the Lesser Banishing Rituals of the Pentagram and Hexagram all these years do you really think it has done anything at all for you?

I guess we never really have proof do we? lol lol

Name withheld

....

Hi Name withheld,

You're absolutely right! We can never prove anything like that. Who knows? In the 1960s and 1970s my brother and I were both radical left-wingers. I started banishing around 1974—he didn't. Now he's a full blown right-winger, but I'm still a shameless lefty. Did my banishing rituals protect me from demons Rush Limbaugh and Glenn Beck? Who knows!

Many of my friends from high school are dead. Did my banishings keep me from so far sharing their fate? Who knows!

I'm nearing retirement age and I still have no visible means of support. Have my Star Ruby banishing rituals kept riches from my door? Who knows!

Seriously, I banish to set the stage for other magical operations. It gets me in the head space for further work. I view it just like that—just like I've learned to unzip my zipper before I take a piss. Sure there are other ways to get my John Thomas out, but unzipping the zipper is a tried-and-true preliminary to piss work. Then again, what's to prevent me from just letting go with my pants on?

My best,

Baba Lon

✷

Nightmarish Astral Projections

Dear Baba Lon,

I wasn't sure who I could turn to for answers about something that happened to my wife last week. She is still a little shook up by the event and I was hoping that you might be able to provide some answers (or at least potentially direct us to someone).

My wife had learned a form of Kabbalistic meditation a couple of months prior to the trip and had become interested in spiritual pursuits in the last year or so. While we were touring Jerusalem she was feeling really low. She told me she was frustrated because she never felt anything during meditation, prayer, or when she walked through some of the sites that are considered holy by many different groups, and that it all felt empty to her.

Now, she has always been very tolerant of me and my crazy attempts at mystical shenanigans. She told me that some of the experiences I have had just couldn't happen to a girl like her.

So that night in the Holy City I prayed that she be touched by the Divine (she couldn't hear me). She also prayed and asked to be shown some kind of sign or guidance (I didn't know this at the time). During the night at 3:15 in the morning she touches me on the shoulder to wake me up. She's terrified and telling me that something is in the room (I had never seen her scared like this before). So of course I get up quite calmly, turn on the light, and use the bathroom. I don't see anything or feel anything in the room.

She then proceeds to tell me what happened (that night she only gave me a very short sketch because she was so frightened). She had trouble falling asleep, which is very unusual for her. She can normally fall asleep anywhere, unlike me.

While she was laying there listening to all the creaks and things of the hotel, she suddenly felt this rush of energy/force (for lack of a better word) that hit her torso and made her dizzy and very sweaty. The force then started radiating up and down her body (it wasn't painful). She then curled up into the fetal position and buried her head in the pillow. At that point she said she felt like she was in a whirlwind like everything was swirling. There were muffled, soft voices at the moment everywhere from in front, behind, and on all sides talking very quickly, but she couldn't make out any of the words (she described it like voices that you hear while you're underwater). Then she tried to move again to touch me and discovered that she couldn't. She was paralyzed. Then something touched her right hip, which she described as a feeling like a thin laser that burned and penetrated. After it pulled away from the hip spot it then went into her shoulder and burned progressively more and deeper until it pulled back. Once it pulled out everything began to lessen (voices, swirling, etc.) and then she was able to move and wake me up.

Any insight would really be appreciated.

Sincerely,

Name withheld

P.S. The new *Enochian Vision Magick* book is fantastic.

....

Hi Name withheld,

Glad you like *Enochian Vision Magick*!

This sounds very much like the phenomena that surround a near-wake astral projection—one in which the astral (I hate that word but I'm going to have to use it) body (and its senses) stay for the most part trapped in the restless and distressed physical body. Like when you're too tired to stay awake and too uncomfortable (for one reason or another) to really sleep. This happens to me a lot, so I really recognize the symptoms.

During a natural and successful nocturnal projection (*i.e.*, when you "dream" you are flying, etc.), the astral body escapes at a time when the physical body is relaxed and comfortable enough to stay out of the way. The "astral" body (and your center of consciousness) then easily slips to a relatively high and pleasant level of the particular "plane" of consciousness that resonates to that subtle body. (Just as the physical body and our center of consciousness are comfortable in the material plane ... so too our various subtle bodies are comfortable in their planes.)

However, when the physical body and mind are disturbed or stressed or over-stimulated, the astral body (and its senses) tries to escape but cannot slip out easily and finds itself struggling in the very lowest plane of the "astral" which is more or less the graveyard of the astral plane where all the "corpses" (shells/qliphoth) of all the neighborhood subtle bodies (once inhabited by "living" consciousnesses who have since moved on in bodies of higher frequencies) settle like sediment on the ocean floor. I can imagine the astral graveyard "neighborhood" of Jerusalem is a pretty colorful place!

There's enough remaining "energy" in these corpses to give them the appearance of life, and this plane is filled with mindless creaks and knocks and groans and voices ... it's really quite frightening. All this is almost always accompanied by discomfort, even pain, in one or more of the chakra centers. This is because we exit the body from the various chakras ... each leading to a different plane. For instance, in a successful projection where we find ourselves "flying," we usually have a tingling or thrill in the pit of our stomach (the solar plexus chakra). Other times we pop out from other places. But in a case like this, we're prevented from popping out and the attempt is painful, and real electrical energy (like fire) gets short-circuited and pushed around all over the body (which is usually completely paralyzed for the moment). It hurts and can really freak a person out. What's extra freaky is the fact that often we think that all this is being "done" to us by those noisy, fearsome corpses (who, in all fairness, are really just innocent bystanders in *our bummer*). It's an unpleasant place to hang out, but it's not really dangerous unless you ascribe undo importance to it and give it more energy than it deserves. I've learned to recognize what's happening and relax.

I'm not saying this is what your wife experienced ... but it sounds like it.

Hope this has been helpful, and that you will forgive me for not having more time to address this further, but I'm extremely busy this summer (in general) and this weekend in particular.

My best,

Baba Lon

✷

Baba Lon's Bible Rant

Dear Baba Lon,

I hope that you won't find this a foolish question and yet if you do, I ask that you please be kind. With that said, I would like to share with you something that I recently posted:

> *Is there a difference between what we consider to be God and what we consider to be Lord God? Although I am a Luciferian, I find a lot of food for thought when I read certain sections of the Bible; for instance, in the first few chapters of Genesis. In chapter one, we read how God Created Man in their own image; "Let us make man in Our image, according to Our likeness …" and later, in the same chapter; "See, I have given you every herb that yields seed which is on the face of all the earth, and every tree whose fruit yields seed; to you it shall be for food."*
>
> *Yet in chapter two, Lord God comes into play and creates a garden and places the man(golem?) he created in this garden and says; "Of every tree of the garden you may freely eat; but of the tree of the knowledge of good and evil you shall not eat, for in the day that you eat of it you shall surely die." And only then did Lord God supposedly create woman, not as an equal, but only as a helpmate.*

In chapter one, it is written; "So God created man (mankind) in His (It's [male/female]) own image; in the image of God He created him(self?); male and female He created them." So it seems that there are a lot of contrasts between these two chapters, not to mention chapter three. First of all I would like to mention that Satan and Lucifer are not synonymous (at least from my perspective as a Luciferian). So, in chapter three, a new character comes into play; the serpent (Lucifer) comes to the Woman (and remember that this is Lord God's creation and not God's creation (There is in my opinion a great difference between 'Lord God' and 'God.') and entices her to eat of the tree of knowledge of good and evil saying, "You will not surely die. For God knows that in the day that you eat of it your eyes will be opened, and you will be like God knowing good and evil."(This, I believe, was the original plan to start with.) Later on, Lord God finds out (If Lord God is supposed to be the same as God, wouldn't he know ahead of time what would happen if he put the tree of knowledge of good and evil in the garden in the first place and if so, why did he put it there?) that the woman had eaten of the tree and shared this with the man.

Lord God was angered at the man and woman and cast them out of this garden. The serpent was cursed by Lord God (this is the possible reason why the serpent is considered evil by western society because the churches say that the serpent is the cause for the fall of man. To me, the serpent represents the independence of man to think for himself free of any constricting forces such as the church, government and the wishful fantasies of those that don't know how to read. The serpent is in a lot of cultures, a symbol of wisdom. God is the symbol of perfection something to emulate and become ourselves, after all we are created in the image of God.

Lord God represents subservience to something outside of us, mostly the will of others who use fear and greed to manipulate the masses for their own purposes.

But I digress. Getting back to the subject at hand, I would like to mention that man and woman did eventually grasp the tree of life. Lucifer taught them in the garden and in chapter four, the woman bore two sons. The first son was sired by Lucifer and the second son was that of the man. By the way, in the gnostic gospels Jesus says to one of his disciples; "It was I that moved the woman to eat ..." You can read about that yourselves.

One last thing. "I, Jesus, have sent My angel to testify to you these things in the churches. I am the root and offspring of David, the Bright and Morning Star." Rev. 22:16

In essence, the act of eating the fruit of the tree of knowledge of good and evil represents the remembrance of our own Godhood.

However, this of course is a metaphor of deeper meaning than many would suppose, so I would encourage the readers of the above post to pull out their dusty bibles, and to study the deeper implications and not to just gloss over the material. I believe we can learn from the myths that were passed down to us, we should be aware that these myths are teachings themselves and not just bedtime stories. If we are to learn, we should do more than just scratching the surface.

Lucifer= Light/Darkness in one.

God Bless The Children Of The Beast

Okay, that was the post and I got some interesting replies but nothing that made much sense. I've been reading your book *"Understanding Aleister Crowley's Thoth Tarot"* and have been thoroughly engrossed in the symbolism of the Rose

Cross. Then I came to the page that discusses YHVH and the four suits (by the way, I am aware that the Tetragrammaton represents the four worlds, the four classical elements and so on) and I find this thing gnawing at me from the back of my mind that something just doesn't seem right or at least in a way that makes sense to me. I mean it makes sense to me on a logical level but not necessarily on a spiritual level. Wasn't the Qabalah originally an astrological system that Abraham learned in Chaldea? Maybe I've missed the point completely but I felt that maybe you might be willing to help me to understand the importance of YHVH in the western magical tradition. Though I am not anti Semitic, I am not Jewish either.

I don't believe in God, at least not in the same manner as so many others. I believe that man is God; that God resides in us all; only it is asleep in the same way that most people are ignorant of their own Ignorance. I would like to understand the Qabalah shorn of all the, in my opinion unnecessary religious dross, in which I find it hard to relate.

So, in closing, I would like to congratulate both you and Constance on your celebrating 38th wedding anniversary, and I wish you both many more.

Name withheld

....

Dear Name withheld,

Thanks for the anniversary wishes.

I'm not a bible scholar nor do I intend to become one in my old age. I do know enough about it, however, to make the following observations:

While I personally feel everything is inherently holy, and Truth can be found in anything (including, as the Buddhists point out, in a pile of dog shit) the Bible is, in my opinion, a most unsatisfactory focus for spiritual meditation. As a matter of fact, for me the Bible is neck-n-neck with dog shit.

That being said, if you will go to *Blue Letter Bible* on the internet you can call up individual bible passages side-by-side English and Hebrew. A little digging will show you that the different designations (*i.e.*, God, Lord God, Lord God Almighty, Almighty God, Lord, Lord of Hosts, etc.) are all different Hebrew words. As you've observed, these different designations were probably the author'(s) attempt at differentiating specific aspects of deity or even different deities. Who knows why? Perhaps to unite diverse tribal deities into one super-god. I don't care!

Jewish Kabbalists spend their entire adult lives thinking and arguing about that kind of stuff. That's ok for them. It's their Zen! For most people, however, I believe it is an invitation to mental illness. I can't get beyond the monstrous history of the Bible's compilation, how hideously the text has been (and is continuing to be) used to enslave souls, justify genocidal wars, and establish fanciful land claims. (But tell us how you really feel Baba Lon.)

I'm not anti-Semitic either, but Bible history is not *history* history. No earlier than the sixth century BC does an Israelite nation first begin to emerge upon non-Biblical history. Prior to this, the historical and archaeological fingerprint of a Hebrew nation with its headquarters in Jerusalem is non-existent. There is not one shred of archeological evidence to suggest that the golden kingdoms of David or Solomon ever existed. (Google around if you don't believe me.) Indeed, the first millennium of Jewish history as presented in the Bible has no empirical foundation whatsoever.

Granted, whoever wrote most of the Old Testament (Ezra or Ezra/Nehemiah) in the *sixth* century BC probably did put a bunch of cool Babylonian mystical ju-ju in the text. But most of it was created whole cloth to literally invent a history and a religion for the diverse former captives of what is today called "the Babylonian Captivity." If you don't think things like that happen in the real world just look at the Mormons.

Hope you will please forgive my ranting, but I think it important that you know why I am not inclined to enter too seriously upon a Bible-based discussion.

I suggest you give the Bible a rest for a while. I have written a patently non-biblical book on the Qabalah, called *The Chicken Qabalah of Rabbi Lamed Ben Clifford*[*] and have a DVD out called. *"Qabalah for the Rest of Us."*

Thanks again for writing.

Baba Lon

✷

Binding Spirits Into Objects

Dear Baba Lon,

First the compliment; although I am sure you hear this quite often. Thank you for your wonderful books. I have purchased and read almost all of them; I still need to read your new Enochian Vision Magick[†] along with your previous Enochian Sex Magick[‡] book.

I do have a question that you may be able to help me with. A previous teacher I once had said it is bad form to ask

---

* Lon Milo DuQuette. *The Chicken Qabalah of Rabbi Lamed Ben Clifford: Dilettante's Guide to What You Do and Do Not Need to Know to Become a Qabalist.* (York Beach, ME: Weiser Books, 2001).

† Lon Milo DuQuette, *Enochian Vision Magick: An Introduction and Practical Guide to the Magick of Dr. John Dee and Edward Kelley* (San Francisco: Red Wheel/Weiser, 2008).

‡ Aleister Crowley, Lon Milo DuQuette, Christopher S. Hyatt. *Enochian World of Aleister Crowley: Enochian Sex Magick.* (Scottsdale, AZ: New Falcon Publications, 1991).

a question without expecting to pay. (In short, you should respect the time and effort of anyone who is willing to answer your questions.) So, please accept the gift I sent via PayPal regardless of whether you answer my question or not. Also by no means am I trying to put a "value" on your time. I just want you to know I respect your time and energy.

The question:

I stumbled or was pulled into the occult with the purchase of a "Haunted" ring on eBay.

While I recognize this may sound cheesy this ring was the vessel of a demon which I believed to be genuine. I sent the ring back to the seller for it was still a bit more than I was ready for. Either way this sent me down a path of research and study looking at and continuing to look at different beliefs and theories regarding the occult and psychology, etc.

One thing that seems to elude me is a general overview of how the summoner *binds* a spirit to an item (a bit like the ring I purchased). I have read books regarding thought forms and how to condense them into an object, etc. But I have yet to encounter much if anything written about binding spirits; threatening spirits with holy names (Yes); bargaining with spirits to do your bidding (Yes); but never binding. I was curious if you could suggest a book or had any thoughts.

In your book, *My Life with the Spirits**, you describe summoning and then possibly binding a demon to its sigil and then hiding it in your guitar. Would this simple arrangement of, "I will draw your sigil and protect it if you serve," constitute a binding? Or is there more to it?

I also realize that a lot of overlap exists between the theories of demons being simply subconscious thoughts vs. separate entities. And while I am constantly looking at the different theories, the practical use is always more interesting

* Lon Milo DuQuette, *My Life with the Spirits* (York Beach, ME: Weiser Books, 1999).

(regardless of what is causing it). I guess I don't completely mind if it is all in my head or not.

Also, what are your thoughts in general to familiar spirits being generally bad? generally good? depends, etc.?

Thanks for any help. If however you prefer not to answer my questions that is fine as well.

Thanks

Name withheld

....

Hi Name withheld,

Thanks for the kind words and the very thoughtful and generous contribution to the DuQuette family's life of genteel poverty. I wish I could reward your courtesy with something more substantial than I am about to offer you, because alas, I'm not aware of any particular book to which I can refer you, nor am I able to regale you with a string of personal anecdotes of my personal experiences with binding spirits to objects. I might, however, have some thoughts on the matter and offer an example of something that I have done that might be helpful in your work.

If you have experience in Solomonic magick (conjuring one or more of the seventy-two spirits of the Goetia) you already posses the skills necessary to get the summoning/ trapping part nailed straight away. (If you are not familiar with my take on the subject, please read my recently published *The Key to Solomon's Key*[*] especially the second section).

---

* Lon Milo DuQuette, *Key to Solomon's Key: Is This The Lost Symbol of Freemasonry* (San Francisco: CCC Publishing, Second revised edition, 2010).

The formula of Solomonic magick can also be applied to the conjuration of spirit entities other than the traditional seventy-two spirits outlined in the text. Indeed, it is possible to summon anything into the magick Triangle. Call them 'thought forms' if you will, but if your mind (or the mind of another) can create them, then they are bona fide spirits. I have participated in Solomonic evocations of mythological creatures and fictional literary characters.

Several years ago I was retained to exorcise one of the oldest Catholic Girls Schools in the country (how that came about is a magical story in itself!)*. It seems the staff, students and their families were being beset by a string of particular horrific tragedies; so many in fact that they began to believe it could be nothing less than a case of demonic possession of the school itself. You probably already can guess that I believed it to be something less romantic, yet nonetheless real in its ability to kill and terrify.

Because the attacks were so numerous and varied in nature, I decided I would gather together and focus the dynamics of the entire spectrum of phenomena by creating one master demon who (once I discovered its name) I could summon into the Triangle and using the tried and true techniques of Solomonic magick) curse, banish, and annihilate.

Think of the concept of those little robot toys, *Transformers*, numerous individual tiny robots—but when you put them together they form the fingers and hands and legs and feet and toes and torso and of one big robot. In this case, however, the master demon was made up of a list of tiny demonic units of *whatever it was* that contributed to the car crash that burned alive a teacher and her baby; and *whatever it was* that accelerated the pancreatic cancer of another teacher causing

---

* The detailed story of this operation is in my book, *Low Magick: It's All in Your Head – You Just Have No Idea How Big Your Head Is.* (St. Paul: Llewellyn Worldwide, 2010), 145.

him to die within hours of diagnosis, and *whatever it was* that severed the maintenance man's finger, and *whatever it was* that broke the hip of a teacher, and *whatever it was* that shot and killed the teenaged son of accountant, and *whatever it was* that moved the classroom furniture at night, and *whatever it was* that caused the most beloved young teacher nun to collapse and die in front of a classroom of hysterical students.)

It was quite a night, but worked out pretty well.

I guess what I'm trying to get across is that there are no limits on how you might go about 'binding' a spirit—any spirit—into an object. As the laziest of lazy magicians, I would simply prepare myself to evoke the spirit into the Triangle *a la* my standard Solomonic operating procedures, but I would also place the object itself in the Triangle. When the spirit is trapped in the Triangle it is also trapped in the object.

Using your own ingenuity, figure out a way to magically (or even metaphorically) keep the *object* in the magick Triangle until such a time that you give it license to depart. But (and here's the rub) you will also have to figure out how to keep *yourself* in the magick Circle for the duration of the entire binding period.

Does that thought disturb you? It should. But magicians get used to things like that.

I hope this has been at least a little helpful.

My best,

Baba Lon

✵

Esoteric Enlightenment in Modern Freemasonry

Hi Brother Baba Lon! Got a minute?

A brother at lodge asked me why we don't study the more esoteric aspects of Masonry, like the Tree of Life. I told him that while Masonry is an initiatory rite in an oral tradition like many traditions around the world, it was pretty much a civic thing. I told him some of the appendant bodies touch on the Kabala and some other esoteric work but mostly they run fish fries and walkathons.

I intend to send him a copy of your excellent book, but I got to thinking about his question. It's certainly valid. I know a lot of people think we're sacrificing babies in there and we try and disabuse them of their misconception. But some other people think we're revealing the lost gates of Atlantis and how to levitate rocks out of the quarry.

But some people are expecting something out of masonry it's not delivering: a kind of esoteric education. Perhaps not as thoroughly occult as what (I assume) one gets from the OTO, but something besides civic obligation and architecture. Are these people SOL or is Masonry a) not delivering, or b) holding back?

Fraternally,

Name withheld

....

Dear Bro. Name withheld,

I guess we have to look at Masonry very broadly, like modern academia.

Local Blue Lodges are like grammar schools, complete with PTA meetings, sports activities, bake sales, etc. There is teaching, yes, but only on the most basic and uninspired level. (If there is any genius to be found, it is found bubbling away in a few extraordinary students and teachers who recognize each other and interact in an almost secretive and extra-curricular manner.

Concordant bodies (Scottish Rite, York Rite, etc.) are more like high-schools and community colleges that are basically the same situation as the grammar schools only occasionally there is a half-hearted effort to suggest that there is something further to be discovered for the tenacious and hardworking student. But still, if there is any genius to be found, it is found bubbling away in a few extraordinary students and teachers who recognize each other and interact in an almost secretive and extra-curricular manner.

Masonic Research Societies and esoteric clubs are like the university experience of self-motivated students and teachers. But still, if there is any genius to be found, it is found bubbling away in a few extraordinary students and teachers who recognize each other and interact in an almost secretive and extra-curricular manner.

Masonic Esoteric Work is similar to post-graduate research where the student breaks new ground in the field and in the truest sense becomes master of himself.

At this level the only advantages to being part of the academic system come with the *credentials* (important now only for the advantages that accompany a degree or title) and the association with others who understand and appreciate ones own mastery of the subject and ability to apply that mastery in creative new ways. Here the work is done in the most secretive and patently extra-curricular manner.

At all levels, the work starts and ends with the individual Mason, not his Lodge, Grand Lodge, Concordant Body, or

Research Society. It may take a lifetime to realize how it all related to ones involvement in the Craft.

Fraternally,

Baba Lon

✺

Why Isn't Homosexuality Talked About in Sex Magick

Dear Baba Lon,

I've been reading your books as of late and I love your writing. I guess what I like is your sense of humor. My reason for writing is to ask you why homosexuality isn't talked about in sex magick? I've only seen the subject approached in Secrets of Western Sex Magic by Frater U D. I pretty much agree with what he's written on the subject.

I'm still new to the world of magick and am a reformed born-again Christian. Long story I won't go into. You might say I'm a born-again Magician!

At any rate, I am a gay man and I always enter my spiritual quests cautiously when it comes to homosexuality. Meaning, the last thing I need is to yet again have a group tell me how wrong I am for being gay. A part of me that is unchangeable. It's funny; the Christians believe I chose to be gay. They're half right, I did not choose to be gay, but I do choose to act upon it, not unlike any other sexual being with their preferences. I know, heavy subject!

I really do appreciate your writings; everything is made so much simpler for someone like me who's new to this practice. I feel like magick doesn't have to be hard and your writings pretty much prove that. Thank you so much for contributing to my quest.

Blessed be!!

Name withheld

....

Hi Name withheld,

Thanks for the kind words and encouragement and for taking the time to write. I really appreciate it. Please excuse my brief answer this morning. I've got a lot on my plate today.

Sex magick is for everyone. Everyone who is sexually active and sexually conscious practices sex magick whether they know it or not. In a very real sense it is the magick of creation itself, from sub-atomic particles to events of cosmic proportions. Don't be discouraged that much of sex magick literature focuses upon heterosexual applications and techniques. It doesn't take a great deal of imagination to make the obvious technical modifications for homosexual workings.

The important thing to remember is that, in the final analysis, sex magick is *always a solitary operation.* No matter what the particular object of your operation may be (a new car or spiritual enlightenment) the idea is to *give birth* to that object. To do that you must first make yourself pregnant, and to do that you must dissolve what you think is your individual consciousness in ecstatic union with *whatever* form your beloved takes ... be it the image of a man, a woman, an angel, a tree, a statue, or a painting.

It's easier for heterosexual writers to discuss the theory and practice of sex magick in terms of male/female (give/receive), but everything is essentially the same for the homosexual. Everyone (no matter what ratio of gender orientation they embody) has an opposite and complementary ideal 'beloved' for whom they yearn and with whom they unite during a competently executed sex magick operation. This union triggers the ecstasy of annihilation during which the 'self' of the magician is dissolved into the (for lack of a better word for it) *universal self.* At this moment the magician becomes omnipresent and omnisexual, embodying *everything* and capable of creating *anything* a concentrated will can impress upon the Petri dish of that golden moment.

Sorry to be so brief. Hope this has been helpful.

My best,

Baba Lon

P.S. You might look into the excellent works of my friend Christopher Penczak.

✵

Is Baba Lon a Spy?

Dear Baba Lon,

I really don't expect you to answer this letter. In fact, I'm not sure that I'm not signing my own death warrant by writing you; but I am taking the chance because I strangely trust you more than any other living magician, and I believe that if you answer me you will tell me the truth.

It seems that history is filled with magicians who are spies; John Dee, Cagliostro, Theodor Reuss, Aleister Crowley—and *you.* Are you really a spy? Do you work for the CIA? Is the O.T.O. the Illuminati? I've read in numerous places that you *are*; that you *do*; and that the New World Order is part of the O.T.O.'s program to bring about a one world government. I suppose you've seen the documentaries on YouTube where you are named by name by a former Illuminati member (Name withheld) and whistleblower. He said you are a "Satanist black magician, and a Freemason O.T.O. Illuminati."

This is so confusing to me. You seem genuinely sincere ... even holy. Your books are awesome and you write some of the most enlightening and inspiring things I've ever read about the occult. You seem to have a regular life and family. It's so hard to think of you as evil, or a spy.

I know that there is an Illuminati and that the New World Order is real and that it is evil. I guess if I'm going to be killed for wanting to stop it at least I'd like to know one thing before I die: Who's in charge? Do magicians get recruited by spy agencies, or do magical Orders recruit spies?

Like I said, I don't expect your answer. I guess you already know where I live.

Name withheld

....

Hi Name withheld,

First of all, no. I'm not a spy. I do not work for the CIA, and the O.T.O. has enough on its plate without involving itself in the intelligence community.

That being said, the synchronicities you are observing concerning magicians and spies probably do bend the statistical curve a bit towards the *"I wonder if there's something going on"* side of the scale. I've observed the same thing myself and have an interesting thought that I will never be able to prove or disprove.

It deals with the fundamental consciousness of the individual magician and how the magical environment and the intelligence environment have enough unique qualities in common to bring them together. Both deal with perceptions of reality. Magicians and spies naturally gravitate to one another as flotsams and jetsam of the big ocean—wave of human consciousness.

A few years back I attended a little talk at the International Spy Museum in Washington, DC (don't get any ideas!) that stressed the fundamental job of an intelligence agent is to ascertain "an accurate assessment of what's happening on the ground." Now I know that sounds pretty obvious, but in actuality it is nothing short of metaphysical.

Like John Dee (England's first superspy), people in the intelligence community are striving to determine the most profound and accurate 'reality' of any given situation. If one side's estimation of 'reality' is more accurate than its enemies then they are at an advantage when making proper political or military decisions. It's spying, yes. But it's also a very real form of magick. And it only would make sense for magicians and spies to gravitate toward each other.

Make sense to you?

Baba Lon

PS. I promise I will not kill you or ask any of my Illuminati brothers and sisters to kill you. If you have anything to fear, I believe it is merely the demon of gullibility.

✹

Monday Night Magick Class

Hi Baba Lon,

I have been running tarot classes for a few years. I have been working with tarot for nearly twenty years. I am trying to work out how I can organize my life to run a magick one as well. Can I ask you a few questions about how you manage your

Monday Magick class? If you have time to reply, I would really appreciate it.

How you manage to run a class on anything for twenty-five years?* I am sure there is no end of subject matter, but don't the people drive you nuts? How do you cope with the ones who complain they're not making progress but they don't do the work?

Also, why did you decide to make it a free class? You don't buy into the 'exchange of energies' idea? I assume there are no costs to you, or that you absorb them. I would love to run a free class but there are costs involved for me in terms of room hire, photocopying etc. Money is convenient, but not entirely necessary— I would never, ever turn someone away just because they were broke, but every single 'free' student ends up quitting or just not sticking with it. The excuses become about time, instead of money. What do you make of that?

Thank you :)

Regards,

Name withheld

....

Dear Name withheld,

Please excuse me if this letter is briefer than we would both prefer. I just returned from nearly a month in England and Europe. I'm only half unpacked, and my office is a fire hazard. If I don't straighten it up I won't be able to think worth a damned. So please remember, these words are written by a very tired, disorganized and frazzled hand.

I will try to answer your questions, if a bit out of order.

---

* Baba Lon and Constance have hosted a free weekly magick class in their home since 1978.

How have I been able to manage my Monday Magick class for over twenty-five years?

I don't know, really. Firstly, I can't say that it is 'my' class per se. Class would not be what it is without the efforts and the presence of my dear wife and partner, Constance.

You see, we've always held class in our home … in our living room. It's a casual and intimate event (for as crowded as it sometimes gets). Most attendees have to sit on pillows on the floor, or else perch on the steps to the loft. Average Monday Night Magick class attendance is twelve attendees (a large evening perhaps thirty; a small night five or six).

The mere fact that we hold class in our home establishes a relaxed and respectful atmosphere where I serve more as a host than a teacher, the attendees feel more like guests than students. This keeps everyone on their best behavior.

Constance spends most of the day setting the stage for class (she's a bit of a neat/clean freak), picking and arranging flowers and decorating the living room table with magical items relevant to the night's subject. (During class she will be my most ruthless heckler!)

The ritual 'opening' of class entails the 'passing out of the coasters,' after which Constance serves tea. (This allows a few minutes for late-comers to arrive. Regulars come from as far away as San Diego (eighty-five miles), Lake Elsinore (fifty miles), Los Angeles (forty-five miles), so we try to cut them at least fifteen min. slack.

And now I'm going to jump a bit out of order and talk about why class is free. First of all we do place a donation basket conspicuously near the door. The proceeds from this usually pay for tea. When we have an especially large class, I make sure to remind them that, "Tonight is your opportunity to really make a difference in the DuQuette's income."

I'm not exactly sure what you mean by "the 'exchange of energies idea" but I do know this. A class such as this doesn't serve well as a money making endeavor. I do hold workshops, seminars, and lectures all over the country ... indeed all over the world. I'm the most shameless of self-promoters and I'm not at all above charging plenty for these events, not only to pay my expenses but to help pay my rent. But I open my home once a week because I love magick and I love to teach it, talk about it, practice it, and most importantly (most selfishly), to learn more about it with people I love. If there is an exchange of energy it is certainly to my advantage because I get far more out of class than I give.

Keeping that in mind, you now know why class members don't drive me nuts ... I already *am* nuts. The fact that we don't charge money for class more or less neutralizes any potential complainers. Hell, I can't judge for sure if anyone is making progress or not. I'm not sure I'm supposed to presume to do that. Class goes on, and those who feel they are not getting anything out of it quietly disappear and those who feel they are

FOR Constance . . .
my Beloved.

Merry Christmas 2005 E.V.

Lon

getting something out of it stay on year after year. When I'm out of town or ill it is they who step in and run class

Our class members come from a wide socio-economic band; from struggling musicians on one end of the spectrum, to wealthy business owners on the other. It would put everyone in the wrong frame of mind if I were to charge, say $20.00 per class. It would be too much for the musician (who will stop coming) and not enough for the business owner (who will fall into the trap of thinking he or she is only getting 20 bucks worth of magical education out the class, and will soon move on to other more expensive programs.) By charging nothing everyone sees that what they're getting is priceless. The musician brings his or her friends and the business person (when he or she sees a need) buys us new computers, and builds us a $75,000 temple. (Yes. That really happened!)

I realize our situation is a bit different than yours ... maybe a lot different. But maybe not as much as you think. Either way, for us the secret of a long-running class lies in the fact that we hold it in our own home and make it a highly personal event. Because each class is a mix of absolute newcomers and experienced adepts, I am forced week after week, month after month, year after year (no matter what the subject) to constantly readdress the fundamentals while at the same time bringing provocative new insights to the subject.

It's like ballet class. The adepts have to attend regularly to be constantly reminded of the fundamentals and to stay in shape, the neophytes have to attend regularly to learn the fundamentals and get a chance to work out with (and learn from) seasoned pros.

I hope this has been helpful.

My best,

Baba Lon

✷

Prayer and Enochian Magick

Dear Baba Lon,

I have enjoyed all of your writings. And have learned a great deal.

In your book, Angel Vision, when addressing the Hierarchy, you do not mention using the prayers that Dee used when invoking the angels,

Do you use them? If not, why?

Other Enochian magicians feel that they are very important.

In Light

Name withheld

....

Hi Name withheld,

Thanks for the kind words about my work, but before my head swells too much I have to confess that perhaps you've got me confused with someone else. I am not the author of "Angel Vision".

I do practice (and have for the last thirty years or so) what is often called today "Enochian Magick." I have even written several books of my own on the subject; but the book you mention isn't one of them.

That being said, I strongly urge you to carefully read my book, *Enochian Vision Magick*.* In it I share the fact that I pray

* Lon Milo DuQuette, *Enochian Vision Magick: An Introduction and Practical Guide to the Magick of Dr. John Dee and Edward Kelley* (San Francisco: Red Wheel/Weiser, 2008).

two simple prayers based on Dee's and Kelley's work, to open and close my operations. (I've reproduced these prayers in the book starting on page 192.)

Not to spoil the wonder of discovering things for yourself in my wonderful book (I'm being playful this morning.) but in the text I try to make it clear how Dee and Kelley felt it necessary (and *believing* it to be necessary it *became* necessary) to pray themselves into an altered state of consciousness in order to make contact with the intelligences that would eventually deliver to them a marvelous magical system— a system whose centerpiece is a technique that if used properly offers a much more efficient method of altering consciousness than praying oneself into a stupor.

But please, by all means feel free to pray all you want. Magicians nowadays don't pray enough! Especially if the prayers are real prayers composed in and by your own heart; prayers that give voice not only to *your* deeply felt personal spiritual yearnings and aspirations, but also (and most importantly) prayers that sing of the *love* you feel *for* (and the love you are prepared to receive *from*) the Supreme Intelligence of the Universe.

If other Enochian magicians (especially the ones whose scholarship and experience eclipses my own) disagree with my understanding of this aspect of the system, that's perfectly alright with me. I'm a simple man who is forced to understand things in simple ways. The best I can do as a teacher is merely to share what seems to work for me and hope that others might apply that information to discover what might work for them.

I hope this has been helpful and that you will forgive me if in the future my time might not permit me to take this much time in responding. I'm off to Australia (for 3 weeks!) tomorrow and still have tons of packing to do.

My best,

Baba Lon

✵

Religion and Masonry

Dear Baba Lon,

Thank you for allowing me to pester you with my questions and observations. You are a gentleman and a scholar! (and a Brother Mason!)

I am still trying to figure out what the O.T.O. is all about. I think I am starting to understand that Thelema is actually a religion … correct? *The Book of the Law* is the Thelemic bible in a sense. Thelema is believing that G-d dwells in Man, so that would make Man G-d ... and rather than answering to a higher power, you can be your own G-d by following your will. This would be the absence of a supreme being ... unless you consider yourself a G-d.

I, on the other hand, think that man in a nutshell is a dumb animal and cannot perceive the over all picture that is G-d. A dog can not drive a car, and man can not see his place in the Universe. I am not so sure about Jesus, but he was a great teacher to say the least. I always thought dying on a cross was a small price to pay when you think about all the nineteen-year old kids that died in Vietnam for nothing at all. I would die on a cross to save every soul on the planet ... wouldn't you? People have sacrificed themselves for far less a cause.

I still understand that without some form of organized religion, the world would be a bit chaotic. If some people followed their will, I would have been shot to death by now. I wonder if ignorance is a good excuse for me to get into heaven (if there is one!)?

Name withheld

....

Hello Brother Name withheld,

You're welcome.

Not that I want to sell books (well ... I do!) but I write them to explain things to myself, and in doing so perhaps explain things to others as well. I tried to specifically answer the questions you ask below in "The Magick of Aleister Crowley." (Weiser Books)

But just off the top of my head first thing in the morning I would put it like this:

God is Supreme Consciousness (the Higher–Highest Power) within which all of 'creation' including you and I reside. Everything is an aspect and expression of the Supreme Consciousness. However, just because the sub-atomic particle and the ant, and the tree and you and me are 100 percent Godstuff, it doesn't mean that we have yet raised (or realized) OUR consciousness to the same level as that of the Supreme Consciousness.

Until we have reached that level of self-awareness we are most certainly 'answerable to the higher power' of the Supreme Being and Its Laws (the mechanics of the universe), *i.e.*, you'll be answerable to the mechanics of the universe if you punch me in the nose and steal my lunch ... the "higher power" is likely to reveal Itself to you by allowing me to beat the crap out of you.

I believe you might be missing the point entirely about what 'will' is. "Do what thou wilt" does not mean do whatever you like because you're God. It means you've got a specific job to do as a component in the mind of God. You've manifested in this universe because this job needs (for some reason...God knows what!) to be done on this plane, and it can be done by nobody else but you.

Finding out what that job is and doing it is our personal Great Work. By doing your Great Work you're fulfilling the reason for your existence and bringing yourself into harmony and sync with the Supreme Consciousness ("God's Will").

Your comment on organized religion is well taken. Many people, perhaps most, unanchored by the quest to find their place in the universe, need to be rendered harmless to others (or at least others of their own class and heritage). Organized religions with their laws and authorities serve to frighten and intimidate them into docility. This is most easily done by making the people believe that they are inherently evil and need fixing … something that can only be done by one particular religion.

Masonry, on the other hand, tells us that "...a fund of science and industry is implanted in man for the BEST, MOST SALUTARY, MOST BENEFICENT PURPOSES." We're not evil inside … we just need our rough edges chipped away; our consciousness raised … step-by-step … degree by degree.

Many religions create people who are 'unchaotic' by putting their minds in a prison; Masonry is designed to produce individuals who are free, balanced, productive, creative, loving, and spiritual because their minds have been liberated.

Hope this has been helpful.

Fraternally,

Baba Lon

✸

Magick and Schizophrenia

Letter # 1

Dear Baba Lon,

Is it possible for people with Schizophrenia to better themselves through Qabalistic mysticism?

Name withheld,

....

Dear Name withheld,

I'm sorry to say that I do not believe it would be helpful in most instances.

Sincerely,

Baba Lon

....

Letter # 2

Dear Baba Lon,

I was very distraught over your last reply. I want to ask you a couple more questions. I'm at my wits end and I'm having trouble seeing a reason to continue.

Is it possible for me to look at what I have manifested in my life and discover what my true values are?

How can I discover what my true values are?

Is it possible for me to get better and better myself and make myself fit?

I know that these are dumb questions, but the answers are very important to me.

Name withheld.

....

Dear Name withheld,

I am especially concerned that my reply has put you "... at your wits end and ... having trouble seeing a reason to continue." I'm sorry to have disturbed you to the point of threatening suicide. I was being as frank and as truthful with you as I possibly could, and was hoping you would appreciate my candor.

You asked if I thought it was "possible for people with Schizophrenia to better themselves through Qabalistic mysticism," and I *should* have begun by saying "Anything is possible ... but ... "

I certainly didn't mean to suggest that I believed there were no ways for you to discover your true values or better yourself. But you didn't ask me that!

I certainly didn't mean to suggest that I believed there was not any number of other spiritual disciplines that might (along with proper medical and nutritional treatment) be helpful to you. But you didn't ask me that!

It has just been my observation over the last forty years that heavy involvement in ceremonial/Qabalistic magick exacerbates and amplifies problems and issues associated with Schizophrenia rather than helping, and often contributes to further and more severe levels of self-delusion.

I am not a mental health expert, and I admit that it is possible the conclusions I have drawn from these observations are incorrect. You, of course, might also be the exception. But I would be less than a faithful correspondent if I were to lie to you about my past observations and encourage you do dive deeper into the exercises of Qabalistic thought (the connecting of everything in heaven and earth with every other thing in heaven and earth) which is a process that in its own way represents a self-induced form of mild Schizophrenia.

I wish you the very best of luck and good health.

My best,

Baba Lon

✷

The Qliphoth

Dear Baba Lon,

Can you tell me the correct spelling of the name of "the world of unbalanced forces," "the world of shards," formed when the Sepheratic "vessels" were shattered by the "lightning bolt" descent of "Divine Emanation?" I cannot find it in the index of Scholem's Origins of the Kabbalah which made me pause. Is it a concept in traditional Kabbalah, or only in the western esoteric tradition?

Warmly

Name withheld.

....

Dear Name withheld,

The word is usually rendered in English letters, "Qliphoth." In Hebrew it is spelled:

Q-(Qoph), L-(Lamed), Y-(Yod), P-(Peh), V-(Vau), Th-(Tau)

I would say that the concept of the Qliphoth is old enough to be considered part of the traditional Qabalah.* To the best of my knowledge it has always been, at least in a primitive state, part of the doctrine of the four Qabalistic worlds (which surfaced early in the 12th century with Jacob ha-Nazir's *Masekheth Atziluth* (Treatise on Emanation).

The "shells" are also mentioned in the 25th paragraph of Chapter One of the *Book of Concealed Mystery* the cornerstone of the Zohar, but in this place as part of the "seven inferior emanations of the queen."

In the Qabalah, various seemingly contradictory points of view can all be simultaneously "true." One school of thought may view the entire material universe as the abode of the Qliphoth; another may view it as the averse counterpart of every plane of consciousness (emanation or Sephirah).

My poor brain likes to look things as if *everything* is the Qliphoth ("crust" I call it) of the plane (level of consciousness or being) just above it, *i.e.*, the physical body is the *crust* of the mind, the mind is the *crust* of the spirit (whatever that is!), the spirit is the *crust* of the *one-big-universal-whatever it is.*

Hope this has been helpful.

Baba Lon

---

* It is just my personal preference to spell Qabalah [the root in Hebrew being Q-(Qoph), B-(Beth), L-(Lamed)]. Today we often see the more orthodox prefer "Kabbalah", the Christian mystics like "Cabalah" and those influenced by the Golden Dawn prefer "Qabalah."

✵

Can I Have A Vasectomy and Still be a Sex Magician?

If I may be permitted, I have a question to ask.

You may choose to ignore this question and I will not be offended in the least if you do.

However, I feel that you may be the best person to come to in regards to this question, as you are one of the most knowledgeable people on the subject and certainly the most accessible, and I would be remiss if I were not to at least ask you.

I am curious if getting a vasectomy can cause sexual based magickal operations to be rendered ineffective due to the lack of the spermatozoon. Causing a sort of magical impotency (or perhaps infertility would be a better word), or is the physical cells an unnecessary part of the equation?

Any answer (even if it's &*$@ off) will be much appreciated

Name withheld

....

Dear Name withheld,

Excellent question; and I will give you my answer based on my current understanding of things (even at my age I'm learning and changing my mind all the time!)

First of all, there are certain "sexual based magical operations" that a vasectomy WILL render ineffective or highly problematic. They include:

Workings in which the object of the operation is to become the biological father of a child;

Workings in which the object of the operation is the fertilization of a human egg;

Workings in which the object of the operation involves magically charging or otherwise altering a living sperm cell;

Any working that would require the male operator to believe with unshakable conviction that his body is presently capable of producing and issuing live sperm cells;

Any biological, chemical, or alchemical procedure or experiment requiring one's own living sperm cells.

Other "Sex Magick" operations (which in my opinion is most of them), in which semen (either by itself or in combination with other substances) is used as a medium, material base, or talisman should not be effected by your vasectomy unless your anxiety and doubts over the matter cloud or otherwise distract your ability to concentrate on the object of the operation.

I hope this has been helpful.

Best of luck with your practice!

Baba Lon

✳

Where Am I on the Tree of Life?

Dear Baba Lon,

I know you must be busy, but if you have a couple of minutes, can I ask something? I was introducing a friend to the subject of the relation between the Paths and the Tarot, and she asked me a question I'm still having a tough time trying to answer. Do we go through different paths at different times in our lives; are we on a fixed path until our evolution takes us to the next in order? Or are we on a particular Sephirah during a fixed period in life as our current "base of operations", and from there experience the rest of the paths until we move to the next Sephirah? Also, is there a specific tarot spread that can answer that?

I feel a bit frustrated because after all these years reading about the subject, I have such a hard time trying to answer this question! :(

Name withheld

....

Hi Name withheld,

"Little questions" seldom demand little answers. Don't be surprised if you see this published someday. :-)

Perhaps the reason you are frustrated and having a hard time with these questions is because they are perhaps the most fundamentally 'good' questions a person could ask about this subject, and because ultimately we won't properly know the answers until we experience the very illumination these Qabalistic practices and meditations are designed to trigger. Until we've reached the destination I believe we are not equipped to have more than just a partial and unsatisfactory understanding of the journey.

My grasp (or non-grasp) of the matter is this: First of all, the answer to each of your questions is both and simultaneously 'yes' and 'no'.

Let's start with the assumption that the ultimate nature of being is *consciousness*; that ultimately everything—matter, energy, thought—even existence and non-existence are all aspects of consciousness.

Next, let's for the moment assume that the Tree of Life represents the entirety of this consciousness.

The Qabalists assume that human beings have (or are capable of developing) the spiritual equipment to be the perfect reflection of this totality of consciousness.

The Sephiroth represent ten major landmarks of this consciousness, the lower on the Tree, the lower the vibratory frequency of consciousness.

The Paths that join the Sephiroth are literally the consciousness equivalent to the nerves, sinews, arteries, vessels, that pass influences to and from one or more of these frequencies of consciousness; they are the inner workings of this machine.

In other words, if each of us were fully 'awake' we would realize that we are already enlightened, already the perfect image of this absolute consciousness—NUMBER ONE!

But most of us are not fully awake. (I certainly am not!) Neither are we fully asleep. The level of consciousness we currently identify with most solidly (having provided ourselves with a firm foundation by mastering the levels beneath us) at any given moment could be viewed as our "initiatory" level or degree. There are seasons of our lives when we firmly are entrenched and seasons where we have moments when we backslide and seasons when we glimpse higher levels. There are even times when we momentarily pop into the very highest of consciousness frequencies without having, as it were, 'passed through' the intermediate levels. (Such cruelly tantalizing moments they are!)

I'm probably not explaining this very well. Maybe it's best just to say that the Great Work is doing whatever it takes — grow however we need to grow—evolve however we need to evolve to identify our "self" with progressively higher and higher levels of consciousness. (To get an idea of what I'm talking about, try to remember your spiritual world view of 15 years ago. Then imagine projecting the 'you' of today back into that world. Would you feel a bit like a moron? Would you feel like you had a lobotomy? Would you trade consciousness places with that moron?)

All that things such as the Tree of Life and tarot cards do is offer little tools– little tricks that provide a vocabulary and a filing system to organize your particular route for this journey. The map isn't the journey and everybody's journey is a little different. Our destination however is the same, and it is my firm conviction that we all say the same thing at the end of the journey.

"Shit! I've been here all along."

Baba Lon

Reincarnation

Reincarnation is a big topic, and of course Baba Lon has his opinions. Most of the letters I've received over the years that treat on this subject are from people who believe they are the reincarnations of recognizable historical characters like Aleister Crowley, MacGregor or Moina Mathers, Laylah Wadell, Jack Parsons, Cagliostro, or Jesus Christ. One fellow told me he doesn't remember hardly any details of his life as Aleister Crowley, but if I would tell him a bit about Crowley's life he would be "happy to remember."

Entertaining as these letters can be they are also sad reminders of why the romance of magick can be an unhealthy obsession for people who are disturbed, unbalanced, or otherwise CRAZY to begin with! Needless to say, I leave nearly all these letter unanswered.

The following letter does not fall into the 'occult crazy' category. (My answer, however, might!) It brings up provocative points concerning reincarnation that still tantalize and intrigue me today.

✻

Reincarnation Tree

Dear Baba Lon,

In your autobiography, *My Life with the Spirits*,* you briefly mention your early childhood (infant) memories that suggest you were recalling events you might have experienced in

* Lon Milo DuQuette, *My Life with the Spirits* (York Beach, ME: Weiser Books, 1999).

previous lifetimes. Do you believe in reincarnation? If so, do you believe that a magician has to believe in reincarnation in order to work effectively?

The reason I ask is that (maybe mistakenly, maybe not) I feel that I'm the reincarnation of another writer who died when I was five years old and whose biography I know very well. Actually, it felt as though I knew his biography and all his texts even before I've read about him. My question to you is this; could we both have been alive at the same time? Is there ever a doubling of lives? What is the aim of this "reincarnation"?

Thanks in advance for your answer.

Name withheld

....

Dear Name withheld,

Do I believe in reincarnation? The answer is a very qualified "Yes."

Do I believe that it is possible for one person to be present in two bodies at the same time? The answer is also a very qualified "Yes."

Do I believe a magician has to believe in reincarnation in order to work effectively? The answer is a very unqualified, "No."

And now I'll probably make you sorry you opened up this can of worms because I have a few moments this morning to think out loud about this subject. I hope you're comfortable. Perhaps you might like to open a beer or pour yourself a glass of wine because here comes a rambling rant on why I answered two of your questions with a *qualified* 'Yes.'

You are correct. In my book, *My Life with the Spirits,* I write about my infant memories of what I would (later in life) speculate were scenes of a previous incarnation: *i.e.,* trench warfare of World War I; myself living in the Pacific Palisades area of Los Angeles in the late 1920s or early 30s; and a night drive down the Pacific Coast Highway for a lover's rendezvous in Ensenada, Mexico. As I mentioned in the book, I experienced these memory-visions when I was two and three years old (1950-51) during the months I was confined to my crib because of a debilitating bone disease. At the time I had yet to see a movie, watch television, or view any photographs that would trigger or influence such memories.

I also mention in the book that during a particularly dramatic psychedelic experience in the Southern California desert in 1967 my brother Marc and I simultaneously identified ourselves as being two of our father's uncles who lived in the Los Angeles area and who died years before either of us came on the scene. Both uncles were involved in the early motion picture industry, one being for a time the private secretary to producer/director Hal Roach, Sr. The idea that we might indeed be our own great uncles of course raises the possibility that instead of being memories of previous incarnations these impressions might have something to do with genetic memory (if there is such a thing). I might have something more to say about that in a moment.

When I was in college I was hypnotized by a licensed hypnotherapist and 'regressed' to a previous life. I recalled my death which occurred when I fell from a high-wire while attempting to walk a tightrope. Many years later psychic David P. Wilson* (who was completely unaware of my teenage hypnotic adventure) during an Enochian magick skrying session 'saw' me die in a previous incarnation as I fell from a rope or wire that I was attempting to walk on.

---

* David P. Wilson, who wrote under the name *S. Jason Black*, was perhaps the most talented visionary skryer I've had the privilege to work with. He died in 2006.

Of course there is no way for me to prove any of my possible previous incarnations, and frankly even if I could prove that I was my own great uncle (or Jack the Ripper, or Cleopatra) I would still be stuck with the concept that I am now, have always been, and will ever be the incarnation of no one but myself.

Time as we normally perceive is very fragile, and exists only in a very narrow band of the consciousness spectrum. It's so delicate that we break it every time we fall asleep. Have you ever taken what you thought is a short nap only to discover you'd been sleeping for many hours (or the other way around)? If the rules of time can get themselves so messed up during our daily sleep cycle, just imagine how much differently they operate during death consciousness, if there is indeed such a thing.

Quantum physicists are suggesting a particle of matter can be in two or more places at the same 'time.' Is it any more a stretch of imagination to posit one 'thing' can exist simultaneously in two or more 'times?'

That is what I mean when I say I am the reincarnation of no one but myself. It cannot be otherwise. Your affinity with that departed writer is obviously very real. It might not matter at all that you and he were alive for a while at the same time. TIME DOES NOT EXIST! In one respect all of us—past, present and future are alive at the same moment.

In Thelema, immortality is viewed as being nothing more or less than the "consciousness of the continuity of existence." Humor me while I quote from my own book, *Angels, Demons & Gods of the New Millennium.*"*

"... the age-old search for eternal life is really the quest to attain consciousness of the continuity of existence. Immortality is the prize for those who would achieve this

---

* Lon Milo DuQuette. *Angels, Demons & Gods of the New Millennium* (York Beach, ME: Weiser Books, Inc. 1997).

state of consciousness. From this enlightened vantage point, one no longer counts the string of spiraling incarnations as separate, or even sequential, episodes of experience. Rather, they are perceived as projected concurrently—one wall-to-wall reenactment of a single master adventure with specific and recognizable characters, ordeals, and crisis points. These crises are initiations, and the cast of recurring characters who populate this personal epic are our initiating officers."*

It's pretty much useless to try to understand with your mind why you seem to be continuing the work of someone who appears to be someone other than yourself. If it suits your purposes to accept it as a fact, then do so. When you need to go somewhere in a car, you don't waste time trying to reconstruct every minute detail of how the car came to be, or relive the complex history of how the car got into your possession. In order to get to where you're going you need only get into the car and go. It's obvious to me that you believe you are going in the same direction as this person—that your work is the continuation of his or her work. So don't waste time worrying about how your vehicle got here; just get in and go! But go where?

Obviously, "Why am I here?" is the most important question one can ask oneself in this present incarnation. But there are other questions—lots of questions: If I've lived a thousand times 'before' what do those other lives mean to me now? Am I my own ancestors? Is that what ancestor worship (a universal and very popular doctrine) is all about? Is reincarnation just some strange slight-of-hand phenomenon of consciousness ... an inter-dimensional marriage of DNA and quantum physics? If I change myself in the present am I simultaneously changing my past *and* my future selves? Now there's a thought!

---

* *Ibid.* p 129-30.

I hope you don't think me too crazy for what I'm about to share with you. It's a story that seems particularly appropriate to this discussion—especially because of what happened to me this morning. But for the story to make any sense at all, I'm going to have to give you a little background information.

A couple of years ago (at the insistence of my wife) I began taking two or three short walks around the neighborhood each day. The walks have done wonders for my health (my weight has gone from an unhealthy and uncomfortable 310 lbs. down to a cool 175 lbs.), but all the new blood pumping to my brain has done even more for my memory and meditations.

Each morning about half-way through my walk I pass by a modest Costa Mesa residence whose front yard is adorned by five very large and healthy Detura* plants. They are as tall as trees, and kept from the sidewalk by a sturdy brick and wrought-iron fence. Their upper limbs, however, refuse to be contained in the yard and burst over the top of the fence spilling hundreds of dangling *angel's trumpets* just inches above the heads of sidewalk passersby. In full bloom it is really quite a breathtaking sight.

One morning not long ago I lingered a few moments beneath the canopy of down-pointing yellow bells and felt a curious giddiness as I stood there looking up into the deepness of those huge flowers. "They really *do* look like angel's trumpets," I thought; and couldn't help but think that each flower was pouring down on me some kind of magical blessing or benediction.

I don't usually fantasize spiritual communion with plants, and I confess at first I felt a little silly. I quickly went along on my way. But next morning as I headed out for my walk I found

---

* *Datura arborea/ Solanaceae.* Tree Datura, a cousin of jimson weed, devil's trumpet, devil's weed, thorn apple, tolguacha, Jamestown weed, stinkweed, locoweed, datura, pricklyburr, devil's cucumber, hell's bells, and moonflower.

myself looking forward to passing beneath the 'blessing trees.' This time I swear, as I approached they seemed genuinely happy to see me coming. The blossoms swung madly back and forth in the breeze like tolling bells heralding my approach. "This is crazy!" I thought. "Why would these poisonous flower trees be blessing me?"

Things got even crazier. The next day as I paused again in the shelter of the blessing trees one of the biggest and most perfectly formed flower trumpets caught my eye. I lingered on the texture of its golden-yellow skin and followed it back to the bright green pod that holds the bell firmly to the stem; then I followed the stem to its twisted and spiraling branch; then followed that branch to a thicker branch, and that branch down to the main trunk and down into the ground. Then, in my mind's eye, I plunged underground and watched the roots drawing nutrients and life from the soil.

"It's the Earth!" I thought. "The Earth is blessing me!" —an interesting little thought, but hardly a veil-rending revelation.

The next morning I awoke in a strange and melancholy mood. It was one of those dark funks I wallow in when I realize that my life is well half over and that I've a much longer past than a future. "*Why am I here? How much time do I have left in this incarnation to find out what it is and do it?*"

As I set out on my morning walk I tried to comfort myself with the thought that Lon Milo DuQuette's life has been only one of many. Death will routinely come as it has a thousand times before. I will 'black out' like a deeply anesthetized patient, then somehow, somewhere once again I'll come to self-awareness as a screaming baby pissing and shitting all over myself and the poor damned souls who conspired to create for me a new body – and that all this will continue again and again until I get things right.

I stared at the sidewalk but I barely saw it as it raced by under my feet. I was totally absorbed in a vision of the corpses of thousands of me's—centuries of men, women, and children buried in every corner of the Earth—all decomposing on ocean floors, and in forests, and deserts and mountains—ashes and rotting flesh dissolving into the soil and being sucked up by the roots of plants and trees.

Suddenly, without realizing how I got there, I found myself standing under the 'blessing trees' looking up and into the depths of hundreds of angel's trumpets; but this time they spoke to me in a thousand different voices. (I warned you it was going to get crazy.)

"We are *you*—all the *yous*; all your incarnations; every man, woman, and child you've ever been; drawn to this spot from the vessels of the earth into the roots of these trees; here to bless you; to encourage you; to empower you; to plead with you to fulfill our destinies—*your* destiny; to neutralize our collective karmas; to pay the debts we've left unpaid and redeem the rewards we've left uncollected. *You're* so close this time. *You* can do it. *You* can do it in this life. You can do it for us all. Do it for your *self*!"

I don't know how long I lingered under the trees that morning. I clutched the wrought-iron bars and lifted my face to the silent cloudburst of the totality of liabilities and assets—the comic debts and rewards of this life and each and every one of my past lives all focused upon this moment, and all of them now duly registered in the ledger of my being.

For the next couple of weeks I looked forward to passing under the 'blessing trees,' and their 'message' has been a profound and continual background meditation making me profoundly mindful of the opportunity I have to make things right for myself and my 'ancestors'. It would be a real understatement to say this 'illumination' has been for me a life altering experience.

I guess it would be fair to ask me if I believe I'm really going to do it in this lifetime. My answer to you is an unqualified 'Yes' simply because it has *always been this lifetime*. And I believe yours has always been your *this lifetime* too.

Peradventure

I know I probably left you with more questions than answers, but I believe this is a subject we can't wrap our meat brains around. I hope my words have been somewhat helpful.

My best,

Baba Lon

P.S. I almost forgot to mention what happened this morning. Today the 'blessing trees' are completely bare of blossoms … not a single one.

Some Other Titles From New Falcon Publications

Aleister Crowley's Illustrated Goetia
Taboo: Sex, Religion & Magick
Sex Magic, Tantra & Tarot: The Way of the Secret Lover
Enochian World of Aleister Crowley: Enochian Sex Magick
By Christopher S. Hyatt, Ph.D., and Lon Milo DuQuette

Cosmic Trigger 1
Cosmic Trigger 2
Cosmic Trigger 3
Coincidance
The Earth Will Shake
Email to the Universe
Nature's God
Prometheus Rising
TSOG: The Thing that Ate the Constitution
Wilhelm Reich in Hell
The Widow's Son
The Walls Came Tumbling Down
Sex, Drugs & Magick
Quantum Psychology
By Robert Anton Wilson

Info-Psychology
The Intelligence Agents
Neuropolitique
By Timothy Leary, Ph.D.

Healing Energy, Prayer and Relaxation
The Complete Golden Dawn System of Magic
The Golden Dawn Audio CDs
What You Should Know About The Golden Dawn
By Israel Regardie

Rebellion, Revolution and Religiousness
By Osho

The Dream Illuminati
The Illuminati of Immortality
By Wayne Saalman

Monsters & Magical Sticks
By Steven Heller, Ph.D. & Terry Steele

An Insider's Guide to Robert Anton Wilson
Eric Wagner

Shaping Formless Fire
Taking Power
Seizing Power
By Stephen Mace

Aleister Crowley and the Treasure House of Images
By J.F.C. Fuller, Aleister Crowley, David Cherubim,
Lon Milo DuQuette and Nancy Wasserman

Please visit our website at http://www.newfalcon.com